# Transform Binge-Free Living: A Holistic Journey to Lasting Liberation

**Unique Kade**

# Table of Contents

# INTRODUCTION

Embarking on a journey toward binge-free living is like setting sail on uncharted waters, navigating the currents of self-discovery and wellness. Welcome to a transformative odyssey, where we'll explore the intricacies of **compulsive eating,** unravel the tapestry of mind-body connections, and carve out a path toward holistic healing.

In the following pages, we'll delve deep into the causes and consequences of binge eating, uncovering the patterns and triggers that shape our relationship with food. But this is more than a mere exploration of the symptoms; it's a guide to understanding how a holistic approach can steer us toward a life of balance and fulfillment.

Picture this as your roadmap—highlighting the detours and pitfalls and illuminating the scenic routes of emotional wellness, physical activity, and supportive environments. We'll navigate the terrain of meal planning, goal setting, and seeking professional guidance, equipping you with the tools to navigate the twists and turns of your unique journey.

But it's not just about the practicalities; it's about the soulful aspects. In the chapters ahead, we'll explore the spiritual dimensions, dive into culinary pleasures, and embrace mindful reflections. This isn't just a book; it's a companion on your holistic self-care adventure, offering insights, exercises, and the encouragement you need to discover the full spectrum of your well-being.

And as we traverse through each chapter, remember that this isn't a one-size-fits-all guide. Your journey is as individual as you are. It's about empowerment, resilience, and creating a narrative that transforms your life and inspires others. So, let's set sail together—into a sea of self-discovery, healing, and the breathtaking freedom of binge-free living. The horizon awaits, and so does the extraordinary story you're about to unfold.

# CHAPTER 1

## COMPULSIVE EATING

## WHAT IS IT, AND HOW DOES IT AFFECT YOU?

Let's embark on a journey of understanding the intricacies of compulsive eating—a path often fraught with complexities and nuances that touch the core of our well-being.

Compulsive eating, at its essence, goes beyond mere consumption of food. It's a dance with emotions, a stress response, a coping mechanism that transcends the physical act of eating. In these moments, food becomes more than sustenance; it becomes a refuge, a friend, a temporary solace in life's challenges.

**The Emotional Symphony:**

Imagine compulsive eating as an emotional symphony, where each bite resonates with feelings often too overwhelming to articulate. It's the late-night snacking when loneliness settles in or the rapid spoonfuls of ice cream in moments of celebration and joy. Compulsive eating intertwines with our emotional landscape, creating a unique melody accompanying our highs and lows.

**The Impact on Physical and Mental Well-being:**

But how does this intricate dance affect us? The consequences are multifaceted. Physically, it can manifest as weight fluctuations, nutritional imbalances, and various health concerns.

Yet, the impact extends beyond the physical realm, casting shadows on our mental and emotional well-being. Guilt, shame, and a sense of loss of control become constant companions, shaping our self-perception and influencing our relationships.

**A Closer Look at the Vicious Cycle:**

Compulsive eating often establishes a vicious cycle. The emotional triggers lead to overeating, and the aftermath brings a tidal wave of negative emotions.

In response, the cycle repeats, each rotation tightening the grip of this complex web. Breaking free from this cycle requires understanding the roots of compulsive eating and cultivating a holistic approach that addresses not only the symptoms but the underlying emotional currents.

As we navigate the landscape of compulsive eating, we'll shine a light on the shadows, uncovering the triggers and exploring how a holistic perspective can be the lantern guiding us toward a life of mindful, balanced, and binge-free living.

This journey is not about condemnation but understanding—an exploration of self that paves the way for healing and transformation. So, let's step into the terrain of compulsive eating, armed with compassion and curiosity, ready to unravel the threads of this intricate tapestry.

## A HOLISTIC APPROACH

Imagine a journey toward overcoming binge eating, not as a solitary uphill climb but as a holistic exploration—a multi-faceted approach that embraces the mind, body, and soul. Let's embark on this transformative expedition, where the power of holistic living becomes the compass guiding us to a place of balance, healing, and lasting change.

## ★ Understanding Holistic Approach:

At its core, a holistic approach to overcoming binge eating recognizes that we are not just the sum of our parts; we are intricate beings influenced by physical, emotional, and spiritual dimensions. Rather than isolating the act of eating from the rest of our lives, holistic living integrates every facet, creating a tapestry of well-being.

## ★ Mind-Body Connection:

One key element of the holistic journey is acknowledging the profound mind-body connection. Our thoughts and emotions have a tangible impact on our physical well-being and vice versa. By delving into this intricate interplay, we uncover the roots of binge eating, understanding the emotional triggers and patterns that drive our behaviors.

**★ Cultivating Mindfulness:**

Mindfulness is central to the holistic approach—a conscious presence in each moment. Mindfulness invites us to observe our thoughts and feelings without judgment, creating a space for self-awareness and reflection.

In binge eating, mindfulness becomes a powerful ally, helping us break free from automatic, impulsive reactions and fostering a deeper understanding of our relationship with food.

**★ Nourishing Your Body:**

Holistic living extends to the physical realm, emphasizing the importance of nourishing our bodies with wholesome, nutrient-rich foods. It's not about restrictive diets or rigid rules but choosing foods that honor our bodies, providing sustenance and energy. This aspect of the journey celebrates the vibrant, life-giving qualities of food.

## ★ Embracing Emotional Wellness:

A holistic approach invites us to confront the emotional roots of binge eating. It's an exploration of the factors that contribute to our relationship with food—stress, trauma, or unaddressed emotions. We can dismantle the scaffolding supporting binge eating by addressing these emotional undercurrents, fostering a healthier emotional landscape.

★ **Building a Supportive Environment:**

No journey is undertaken in isolation, and overcoming binge eating is no exception. Holistic living involves cultivating a supportive environment—nurturing relationships, engaging with communities that understand and encourage our goals, and seeking resources that align with our holistic vision.

As you navigate this holistic terrain, you will explore practical strategies, delve into the transformative power of self-care, and weave together the various threads that contribute to a life free from the shackles of binge eating. This isn't just a guide; it's an invitation to embrace a holistic approach that honors the entirety of who you are, guiding you toward a future where balance and well-being flourish. So, let the journey begin—one that transcends mere overcoming and leads to a profound and enduring transformation.

You

# THE CAUSES AND CONSEQUENCES OF BINGE EATING

Welcome to this section—a pivotal exploration into the heart of binge eating. In this section, we'll don our detective hats and unravel the intricate threads that weave the tapestry of compulsive consumption.

Join me as we delve into the causes and consequences of binge eating, illuminating the patterns and triggers that shape our relationship with food. It's not just about understanding; it's about forging a path toward mindful living, where awareness becomes the catalyst for lasting change. Let's embark on this investigative journey together.

# IDENTIFYING YOUR BINGE EATING PATTERNS AND TRIGGERS

Binge eating, like a complex puzzle, consists of intricate patterns and elusive triggers. In this chapter, we embark on a journey of self-discovery, equipped with the tools to decipher the blueprint of your compulsive consumption. Understanding the nuances of your binge eating patterns and recognizing the triggers that set the stage for these behaviors are pivotal steps toward lasting change.

**1. Decoding Binge Eating Patterns:**

**A. Time and Routine:**

Examine the timing of your binge episodes. Are they linked to specific times of the day, such as evenings or late nights? Identifying patterns in your daily routine can reveal insights into the cyclical nature of your binge eating.

**B. Emotional Associations:**

Explore the emotional landscape surrounding your binges. Are there recurring feelings of stress, sadness, or loneliness? Unraveling the emotional threads intertwined with your eating patterns is crucial in understanding the deeper motivations behind your behavior.

**C. Environmental Triggers:**

Consider the physical environment where binge eating occurs. Is it associated with specific locations or situations, like being alone at home or social gatherings? Recognizing the environmental factors contributing to binge episodes sheds light on external influences.

## 2. Unmasking Triggers:

### A. Emotional Triggers:

Dive into the emotional triggers that propel you toward binge eating. Are there unresolved emotions, traumatic experiences, or unmet needs? Identifying emotional triggers involves introspection and a willingness to confront the root causes of your relationship with food.

### B. Social and Peer Influences:

Reflect on the role of social dynamics in your binge eating patterns. Are there specific social situations or peer interactions that trigger episodes? Understanding the influence of external factors can empower you to navigate social environments more mindfully.

**C. Restrictive Dieting and Deprivation:**

Explore any history of restrictive dieting or periods of food deprivation. Binge eating can often be a reaction to prolonged restriction. Recognizing these patterns helps break the cycle and fosters a more balanced and sustainable approach to nutrition.

## 3. Keeping a Binge Diary:

Start a binge diary to track episodes, emotions, and circumstances surrounding your eating habits. This tool is a valuable companion on your journey, providing a tangible record that enhances self-awareness and facilitates discussions with healthcare professionals or support networks.

## 4. Seeking Professional Guidance:

Consider consulting with healthcare professionals, therapists, or nutritionists who specialize in binge eating disorders. Their expertise can offer valuable insights into your patterns and triggers, providing tailored strategies for intervention and support.

## HOW BINGE EATING IMPAIRS YOUR PHYSICAL AND MENTAL HEALTH

In this exploration, we delve into the profound impact of binge eating on both your physical and mental health. Binge eating, more than a mere indulgence, can cast a wide-reaching shadow, affecting the body and the intricate tapestry of the mind. Let's dissect the nuanced ways in which this compulsive behavior impairs your overall well-being.

### Physical Consequences of Binge Eating

### 1. Weight Fluctuations:

Binge eating often leads to significant weight fluctuations, creating a cycle of gain and loss that can strain the body's natural equilibrium. This constant yo-yo effect can contribute to metabolic irregularities, putting additional stress on the cardiovascular system.

### 2. Nutritional Imbalances:

Compulsive consumption tends to be high in calorie-dense, low-nutrient foods. This can result in nutritional imbalances, deficiencies, and inadequate intake of essential vitamins and minerals, jeopardizing the body's ability to function optimally.

### 3. Gastrointestinal Distress:

The sheer volume of food consumed during binge episodes can lead to gastrointestinal distress. Issues such as bloating, indigestion, and discomfort become common companions, impacting physical well-being and emotional distress.

## <u>Mental Health Ramifications</u>

### 1. Emotional Turmoil:

Binge eating is often accompanied by a rollercoaster of emotions—guilt, shame, and a sense of loss of control. These emotional upheavals can contribute to heightened anxiety and depression, forming a detrimental feedback loop that exacerbates the binge eating cycle.

### 2. Low Self-Esteem and Body Image Issues:

The physical consequences of binge eating can lead to low self-esteem and negative body image. The societal stigma attached to weight gain may further compound these issues, fostering a challenging environment for mental well-being.

### 3.  Isolation and Withdrawal:

As binge eating becomes a coping mechanism, individuals may withdraw from social situations, leading to isolation. The shame associated with the behavior can create a barrier to seeking support, perpetuating a cycle of loneliness and mental distress.

## <u>Impact on Cognitive Function</u>

### 1.  Brain Fog and Fatigue:

The physiological effects of binge eating extend to cognitive function. Blood sugar fluctuations and nutritional imbalances can contribute to brain fog and fatigue, affecting concentration, memory, and overall mental clarity.

## 2. Disrupted Sleep Patterns:

Binge eating, especially during late-night episodes, can disrupt sleep patterns. Poor sleep quality and irregular sleep cycles contribute to mood disturbances and impair cognitive performance during waking hours.

## <u>Breaking the Cycle</u>

Recognizing the profound impact of binge eating on physical and mental health is the first step toward breaking the cycle. Seeking professional help, building a support network, and adopting holistic strategies that address the physical and emotional aspects are essential components of the journey toward recovery.

## <u>Conclusion</u>

In summary, identifying binge eating patterns and triggers is a powerful tool for transformative change, offering a foundation for mindful, balanced, and binge-free living. Recognizing the multifaceted toll on physical and mental health underscores the need for compassionate healing and acts as a catalyst for positive change. This journey toward holistic well-being is illuminated by self-awareness, resilience, and the promise of a healthier future, providing the groundwork for an empowered and transformative path ahead.

# CHAPTER 2

# THE MIND-BODY CONNECTION IN BINGE-FREE LIVING

Welcome to a chapter that transcends the boundaries between mind and body—a realm where the intricate dance of thoughts, emotions, and physical sensations converges. In "The Mind-Body Connection in Binge-Free Living," we journey to unravel the profound interplay between our mental and physical realms. Here, the pursuit of binge-free living takes on a holistic hue, emphasizing the integral connection between our thoughts, emotions, and the well-being of our bodies. Join me as we explore the transformative power of nurturing harmony within, paving the way for a life liberated from the shackles of compulsive consumption.

# HOW HOLISTIC NUTRITION SUPPORTS YOUR HEALTH AND WELL-BEING

In this exploration, we dive into holistic nutrition—a cornerstone in the journey toward overall health and well-being. Holistic nutrition extends beyond mere dietary choices; it's a lifestyle that recognizes the interconnectedness of mind, body, and spirit. Let's unravel how holistic nutrition can nourish and support your entire being.

**1. Understanding Holistic Nutrition:**

**A. Whole Foods Philosophy:**

The commitment to whole, unprocessed foods is at the heart of holistic nutrition. These nutrient-dense choices provide the body with a spectrum of vitamins, minerals, and antioxidants, fostering optimal function and resilience.

### B. Mindful Eating Practices:

Holistic nutrition encourages mindful eating—a practice that involves savoring each bite, listening to your body's hunger and fullness cues, and cultivating a deeper connection with the act of nourishment.

## 2. Balancing Macronutrients:

### A. Protein for Sustained Energy:

Holistic nutrition emphasizes the importance of balanced macronutrients. Protein, in particular, is crucial in providing sustained energy, supporting muscle health, and contributing to an overall sense of vitality.

**B. Healthy Fats for Cognitive Function:** Healthy fats, such as avocados, nuts, and olive oil, are integral to holistic nutrition. These fats support cognitive function, aid nutrient absorption, and contribute to the body's cellular integrity.

**C. Complex Carbohydrates for Stability:** Holistic nutrition advocates for complex carbohydrates—whole grains, fruits, and vegetables—that provide a steady release of energy, stabilize blood sugar levels and promote sustained mental and physical well-being.

**3. Personalized Nutrition Plans:**

**A. Tailoring Nutrition to Individual Needs:** Recognizing that each person is unique, holistic nutrition emphasizes personalized plans.

Consideration is given to factors such as age, lifestyle, and health goals, ensuring that nutritional choices align with individual needs.

B. **Integrating Traditional Wisdom:**

Holistic nutrition often integrates traditional and cultural wisdom regarding food. This can include incorporating locally sourced, seasonal produce and drawing on traditional practices that have stood the test of time.

## 4. Supporting Gut Health:

### A. The Gut-Brain Connection:

Holistic nutrition recognizes the intricate relationship between gut health and mental well-being. A healthy gut microbiome contributes to a balanced mood, cognitive function, and overall emotional resilience.

### B. Probiotics and Prebiotics:

Incorporating probiotic-rich foods and prebiotic fibers is a key tenet of holistic nutrition. These support the growth of beneficial gut bacteria, promoting digestive health and fortifying the immune system.

**5. Cultivating Mindful Eating Practices:**

**A. Intuitive Eating:**

Holistic nutrition aligns with the principles of intuitive eating—an approach that encourages tuning into your body's natural hunger and fullness signals, fostering a healthy relationship with food.

**B. Mind-Body Connection:**

By embracing holistic nutrition, you nurture the mind-body connection. The foods you consume affect physical health, mental clarity, emotional stability, and spiritual well-being.

# HOW MINDFULNESS CAN ENHANCE YOUR EATING EXPERIENCE AND SATISFACTION

In this chapter, we embark on a journey that transcends the act of eating—it's an exploration of mindfulness. This practice transforms simple nourishment into a profound and satisfying experience. Let's delve into how mindfulness can elevate your relationship with food, enhancing not just the flavors on your plate but the satisfaction derived from every bite.

**1. The Essence of Mindful Eating:**

**A. Present Moment Awareness:**

At the core of mindful eating lies the practice of present-moment awareness. It involves fully engaging with the sensory experience of eating—savoring the flavors, textures, and aromas without the distraction of external stimuli.

## B. Cultivating a Non-Judgmental Approach:

Mindfulness encourages a non-judgmental attitude toward food. It's about observing thoughts and feelings without attaching labels of "good" or "bad," fostering a compassionate and guilt-free relationship with what you eat.

## 2. The Mind-Body Connection in Mindful Eating:

### A. Listening to Hunger and Fullness Cues:

Mindful eating involves tuning into your body's hunger and fullness cues. By paying attention to the subtle signals, you can foster a more intuitive and responsive approach to when and how much you eat.

## B. Recognizing Emotional Triggers:

Mindfulness extends beyond the physical act of eating—it invites you to explore the emotional landscape surrounding your food choices. By recognizing emotional triggers, you gain insight into emotions' role in your relationship with food.

## 3. The Ritual of Mindful Eating:

### A. Creating a Sacred Space:

Transform your mealtime into a ritual by creating a sacred space for eating. This might involve setting a beautifully arranged table, eliminating distractions, and approaching your meal with gratitude.

### B. Slow and Deliberate Eating:

Mindful eating embraces the art of slow and deliberate eating. Soring each bite heightens the sensory experience and allows your body to register fullness more effectively.

## 4. Mindful Practices Beyond the Plate:

### A. Mindful Meal Preparation:

Extend mindfulness to the preparation of your meals. Engage in cooking with awareness, appreciating the ingredients, and infusing your culinary creations with intention.

### B. Gratitude and Reflection:

After the meal, take a moment for gratitude and reflection. Acknowledge the nourishment you've received and the effort that went into bringing the food to your table, fostering a sense of appreciation.

## 4. Mindful Eating and Nutritional Health:

### A. Improved Digestion:

Mindful eating has been associated with improved digestion. Reducing stress during meals and enhancing awareness of the eating process contribute to better nutrient absorption and overall digestive well-being.

**B. Weight Management:**

Mindfulness can play a role in weight management by promoting a healthier relationship with food. You're better equipped to make balanced and satisfying food choices by being attuned to your body's needs and cues.

## Conclusion

In the pursuit of binge-free living, holistic nutrition and mindfulness intertwine as powerful allies. Holistic nutrition transcends diets, offering a lifestyle that nurtures the whole self. Simultaneously, mindfulness transforms eating into a fulfilling experience, fostering a deeper connection with each bite. This journey is not just about what you eat but an invitation to a lifestyle that supports overall well-being—an exploration leading to a heightened appreciation for flavors and the profound satisfaction found in every mindful moment.

# CHAPTER 3

# EMOTIONAL WELLNESS AND BINGE-FREE LIVING

Welcome to the heart of the journey—Chapter 3: Emotional Wellness and Binge-Free Living. This chapter delves into the intricate landscape of emotions, unraveling the ties that bind them to compulsive eating. It's about understanding the emotional roots and cultivating a space for healing and resilience. Join me as we explore the transformative power of emotional wellness, paving the way for a life liberated from the emotional triggers that weave the fabric of binge eating.

# HOW TO ADDRESS THE EMOTIONAL ROOTS OF BINGE EATING

In this section, we embark on a poignant exploration, peeling back the layers to understand and address the emotional roots of binge eating. It's a journey of introspection, compassion, and resilience—an endeavor to unearth the emotional triggers contributing to compulsive consumption. Let's delve into the comprehensive strategies that empower you to confront and heal the emotional roots woven into the fabric of binge eating.

## 1. Cultivating Self-Awareness:

### A. Mindful Reflection:

Start by engaging in mindful reflection. Create a safe and non-judgmental space to explore your emotions, recognizing patterns and triggers without criticism. This self-awareness forms the foundation for addressing the emotional roots of binge eating.

### B. Journaling Practices:

Utilize journaling as a therapeutic tool. Documenting your thoughts and feelings provides:

★ A tangible record.

★ Allowing you to identify emotional patterns.

★ Shifts.

★ Connections to your eating behaviors.

## 2. Identifying Emotional Triggers:

### A. Recognizing Stressors:

Uncover the stressors in your life that may be contributing to binge eating. Identifying these triggers is crucial in addressing their emotional impact, Whether work-related pressure, relationship challenges, or other external stressors.

**B. Exploring Past Trauma:**

Delve into your past with sensitivity and care. Traumatic experiences can be profound emotional triggers. Consider seeking support from a therapist or counselor to navigate and heal from past wounds that may influence your current relationship with food.

**3. Developing Healthy Coping Mechanisms:**

**A. Mindfulness and Relaxation Techniques:**

Integrate mindfulness and relaxation practices into your daily routine. Techniques such as deep breathing, meditation, and yoga can help you build resilience against stress and provide healthier coping mechanisms.

**B. Emotional Regulation Skills:**

Learn and practice emotional regulation skills. This includes identifying and expressing emotions constructively, fostering emotional intelligence, and developing strategies to manage intense feelings without turning to food for comfort.

**4. Seeking Professional Support:**

**A. Therapy and Counseling:**

Consider therapy or counseling as a supportive resource. A mental health professional can guide you through addressing emotional roots, providing tools for emotional regulation, and offering a safe space for exploration and healing.

**B. Support Groups:**

Engage with support groups or communities where individuals share similar struggles. Connecting with others who understand your journey provides a sense of camaraderie and fosters a supportive environment for emotional healing.

## 5. Building Resilience and Self-Compassion:

### A. Resilience Building Practices:

Cultivate resilience through practices that enhance your emotional strength. This may involve setting realistic goals, embracing a growth mindset, and learning from challenges rather than viewing them as setbacks.

### B. Self-Compassion Exercises:

Practice self-compassion exercises to develop a kinder relationship with yourself. Treat yourself with the same empathy and understanding you would offer a friend facing similar challenges, fostering a foundation for emotional well-being.

# HOW TO BALANCE MOVEMENT WITH REST AND RECOVERY

This section delves into the delicate dance between movement, rest, and recovery—a balance that forms the cornerstone of holistic well-being. It's not just about physical exertion but understanding the ebb and flow that keeps your body resilient and thriving. Let's explore the comprehensive strategies to harmonize movement with rest and recovery, fostering a sustainable and balanced approach to your overall health.

**1. Understanding the Importance of Balance:**

**A. The Role of Movement:**

Acknowledge the benefits of regular physical activity. Movement enhances cardiovascular health, strengthens muscles and bones, and improves overall mental well-being. Recognize that a balanced approach involves not just intensity but also your activities.

**B. The Significance of Rest and Recovery:**
Equally vital is the recognition of the importance of rest and recovery. Rest allows your body to repair and regenerate, preventing burnout and reducing the risk of injuries. It's an integral that optimizes your body functions optimally.

**2. Designing a Balanced Exercise Routine:**

**A. Incorporating Variety:**
Diversify your exercise routine to engage different muscle groups and prevent overuse injuries. Blend cardiovascular exercises, strength training, flexibility work, and activities that

promote balance and coordination for a well-rounded approach.

### B. Tailoring Intensity:

Listen to your body's signals when it comes to exercise intensity. Incorporate both high-intensity and low-intensity workouts to prevent overtraining. Periodization, which involves varying the intensity and volume of your workouts over time, is a valuable strategy for balanced training.

### 3. The Art of Rest and Active Recovery:

### A. Scheduling Rest Days:

Integrate dedicated rest days into your weekly routine. These are days when you allow your body to recover fully, reducing the risk of burnout and promoting long-term sustainability in your fitness journey.

### B. Active Recovery Practices:

Explore active recovery methods on your rest days. Gentle activities such as walking, yoga, or swimming can enhance blood flow, promote flexibility, and aid in recovery without imposing excessive strain on your body.

## 4. Prioritizing Sleep:

### A. Recognizing the Role of Sleep:

Prioritize sleep as a crucial component of recovery. Quality sleep is essential for muscle repair, hormone regulation, and overall well-being. Establish consistent sleep patterns and create a conducive sleep environment to support your body's recovery processes.

### B. Managing Stress Levels:

Address stress as a potential barrier to rest and recovery. Incorporate stress management techniques such as meditation, deep breathing, or mindfulness practices to create a more conducive environment for your body to recover.

## 5. Listening to Your Body:

### A. Tuning into Physical Signals:

Pay attention to your body's signals. If you experience persistent fatigue, soreness, or signs of overtraining, consider adjusting your exercise routine and ensuring that rest and recovery play a more prominent role in your regimen.

### B. Adjusting Based on Life Circumstances:

Be flexible in adapting your exercise routine to life circumstances. Factors such as illness, work stress, or other life events may require adjustments to maintain the delicate balance between movement and recovery.

# **Conclusion**

Addressing emotional roots in binge eating is profound self-care—an invitation to a journey of healing. This expedition empowers you to rewrite your food relationship. Simultaneously, balance movement with rest—a personalized journey aligning with your body and lifestyle.

This chapter guides in cultivating this balance, emphasizing quality recovery. Together, we navigate emotional landscapes and holistic well-being, recognizing the path to binge-free living is paved with self-awareness, compassion, and a harmonious dance between movement and rest—contributing to vitality, joy, and fulfillment.

# CHAPTER 4

# PHYSICAL ACTIVITY AND BINGE-FREE LIVING

Welcome to Chapter 4: Physical Activity and Binge-Free Living. In this chapter, we'll delve into the art of balancing movement with rest—a personalized journey crucial for sustained well-being. Join me as we navigate the terrain of holistic health, emphasizing the quality of both activity and recovery on the path to lasting liberation from binge eating.

How to Find and Maintain an Enjoyable and Sustainable Exercise Routine: A Holistic Approach to Physical Well-Being

Embarking on a journey toward lasting well-being involves not just movement, but the art of cultivating a sustainable and enjoyable exercise routine. This chapter serves as a guide, offering practical insights and holistic strategies to help you discover, embrace, and maintain a form of physical activity that aligns with your unique preferences and lifestyle.

## 1. Exploring Varied Activities:

### A. Assessing Personal Preferences:

Begin by assessing your personal preferences. Consider activities you enjoy or have always wanted to try. Whether it's dancing, hiking, cycling, or yoga, the key is to find joy in movement.

### B. Incorporating Variety:

Embrace variety in your routine. Experiment with different activities to keep your routine engaging. This not only prevents monotony but also targets different muscle groups, contributing to overall fitness.

## 2. Setting Realistic Goals:

### A. Establishing Achievable Milestones:

Set realistic and achievable goals. Start with small milestones that align with your fitness level and gradually progress. Celebrating these achievements fosters motivation and enhances the sustainability of your exercise routine.

### B. Prioritizing Consistency Over Intensity:

Prioritize consistency over intensity. Regular, moderate exercise is often more sustainable than sporadic intense workouts. This approach not only prevents burnout but also supports long-term commitment.

## 3. Finding Joy in Movement:

### A. Connecting with Passion:

Connect with activities that bring you joy. Whether it's the rhythmic flow of a dance class or the meditative quality of a nature walk, finding joy in movement makes exercise a positive and fulfilling experience.

### B. Incorporating Playfulness:

Infuse playfulness into your routine. Engage in activities that feel like play rather than a chore. This could be anything from recreational sports to playful workouts that tap into your inner child.

## 4. Tailoring Exercise to Your Lifestyle:

### A. Integrating into Daily Life:

Integrate exercise into your daily life. Identify opportunities for movement, such as taking the stairs, walking during breaks, or incorporating short workouts into your routine. This makes exercise more sustainable and accessible.

**B. Adapting to Changing Circumstances:**

Be flexible and adapt your routine to changing circumstances. Life is dynamic, and your exercise routine should be adaptable. This flexibility ensures that your commitment to movement remains resilient.

**5. Building a Support System:**

**A. Partnering with a Workout Buddy:**

Consider partnering with a workout buddy. Having a companion not only adds a social element but also provides mutual motivation and accountability. Shared experiences make the journey more enjoyable.

## B. Joining Fitness Classes or Communities:

Join fitness classes or communities. Connecting with like-minded individuals creates a supportive environment and adds a sense of community to your exercise routine.

## 6. Listening to Your Body:

### A. Prioritizing Rest and Recovery:

Prioritize rest and recovery. Listen to your body's signals and allow time for recuperation. Balancing activity with sufficient rest is crucial for preventing burnout and sustaining long-term well-being.

### B. Adjusting Intensity:

Be mindful of intensity levels. It's essential to challenge yourself, but also to recognize when your body needs a break. Adjusting the intensity of your workouts promotes sustainability and prevents overexertion.

# HOW TO BALANCE MOVEMENT WITH REST AND RECOVERY

Achieving holistic physical well-being goes beyond the sheer volume of movement; it involves the delicate art of balancing activity with essential rest and recovery. This chapter serves as a comprehensive guide, offering insights and practical strategies to help you find equilibrium in your fitness journey, preventing burnout and fostering sustainable well-being.

**1. Understanding the Importance of Rest and Recovery:**

**A. Physiological Benefits:**

Recognize the physiological benefits of rest and recovery. During periods of rest, the body repairs and strengthens itself, contributing to improved performance and overall fitness. Understanding this fundamental principle is key to achieving a balanced routine.

**B. Preventing Overtraining:**

Guard against overtraining. Pushing your body without adequate rest can lead to fatigue, increased injury risk, and diminished performance. Prioritizing recovery prevents overtraining and supports long-term physical health.

**2. Establishing a Balanced Exercise Routine:**

**A. Incorporating Different Modalities:**

Incorporate a variety of exercise modalities. Balancing high-intensity workouts with low-impact activities, such as yoga or swimming, ensures diverse stimuli for the body and reduces the risk of overuse injuries.

**B. Structuring Rest Days:**

Structure dedicated rest days into your routine. Allow your body time to recuperate, especially after intense or prolonged workouts. Rest days are integral to preventing burnout and promoting sustained engagement.

### 3. Tailoring Rest Intervals:

**A. Customizing Based on Activity:**

Customize rest intervals based on the type of activity. High-intensity workouts may require longer rest periods, while low-impact exercises might involve shorter intervals. Tailoring rest to the specific demands of your routine optimizes recovery.

## B. Active Recovery Strategies:

Incorporate active recovery strategies. Light exercises, such as walking or gentle stretching, on rest days, can enhance blood circulation, alleviate muscle stiffness, and contribute to overall recovery.

## 4. Listening to Your Body's Signals:

### A. Recognizing Signs of Fatigue:

Be attuned to signs of fatigue. Persistent muscle soreness, decreased performance, or disrupted sleep may indicate your body needs more recovery. Listening to these signals enables you to adjust your routine accordingly.

### B. Adjusting Intensity and Duration:

Modify the intensity and duration of your workouts based on how your body responds. If fatigue persists, consider reducing the intensity or shortening the duration to allow for adequate recovery.

## 5. Prioritizing Quality Sleep:

### A. Sleep's Impact on Recovery:

Acknowledge the role of sleep in recovery. Quality sleep is crucial for physical restoration, muscle repair, and overall well-being. Prioritize consistent and sufficient sleep to maximize the benefits of your exercise routine.

### B. Establishing Sleep Hygiene Practices:

Incorporate sleep hygiene practices. Create a conducive sleep environment, limit screen time before bedtime, and adhere to a consistent sleep schedule. These practices enhance the quality of your rest and aid in recovery.

## 6. Hydrating and Nutrition for Recovery:

### A. Hydration's Role in Recovery:

Recognize the importance of hydration in recovery. Water supports various bodily functions, including nutrient transport and toxin removal. Staying adequately hydrated enhances the efficiency of your recovery processes.

### B. Nutrient-Rich Post-Workout Meals:

Prioritize nutrient-rich post-workout meals. Consuming a balanced combination of carbohydrates, proteins, and healthy fats supports muscle repair and replenishes energy stores, contributing to effective recovery.

## <u>Conclusion</u>

Balancing movement with rest is at the core of holistic physical well-being. From understanding the physiological benefits of recovery to embracing variety in exercise, this chapter guides you in fostering sustainable fitness. It's not just a practice; it's a commitment to lasting vitality, resilience, and overall well-being—a dynamic exploration of movement, joy, and holistic health.

# Chapter 5

## CREATING A SUPPORTIVE ENVIRONMENT FOR BINGE-FREE LIVING

Step into Chapter 5, where we delve into the transformative influence of your surroundings in the pursuit of binge-free living. Beyond individual efforts, the support you receive from your environment, relationships, and community is a powerful catalyst for change. In this exploration, we uncover the strategies to cultivate a nourishing and understanding ecosystem essential for embracing a lifestyle free from compulsive consumption. Join me on a journey of community, connection, and empowerment as we explore the art of creating a supportive environment for your path to balanced and mindful living.

# HOW TO CULTIVATE HEALTHY AND NOURISHING RELATIONSHIPS

In this section, we embark on a profound exploration into relationships—a crucial facet of the journey toward binge-free living. Cultivating healthy and nourishing connections forms the bedrock of emotional support, understanding, and encouragement. Let's unravel the intricacies of building and sustaining relationships that contribute to your well-being and empower your commitment to a balanced and mindful lifestyle.

**1. Prioritizing Communication:**

**A. Open and Honest Dialogue:**

Foster an environment of open and honest communication. Express your feelings, needs, and goals, and encourage your loved ones to share their thoughts. Clear communication lays the groundwork for mutual understanding and support.

### B. Active Listening:

Practice active listening to deepen your understanding of others. Give your full attention, refrain from judgment, and validate the emotions and perspectives of those around you. This cultivates a sense of connection and fosters empathy.

## 2. Establishing Boundaries:

### A. Clearly Defined Limits:

Establish clearly defined boundaries to protect your emotional well-being. Communicate your limits regarding discussions, activities, or behaviors that may trigger or harm your journey toward binge-free living.

## B. Respect for Individual Boundaries:

Respect the boundaries set by others in your relationships. Understanding and acknowledging each person's need for personal space and autonomy contributes to a healthier and more harmonious connection.

## 3. Building a Supportive Network:

### A. Identify Sources of Support:

Identify individuals within your circle who are supportive of your journey. Surround yourself with friends and family who understand your goals and can provide encouragement, empathy, and a non-judgmental presence.

### B. Educate Your Support Network:

Educate your support network about binge eating disorder and your specific needs.

Providing information fosters understanding and equips your loved ones to offer more targeted and meaningful support.

## 4. Nurturing Empathy and Understanding:

### A. Empathetic Responses:

Encourage empathy by sharing your experiences and feelings. Help your loved ones understand the emotional nuances of your journey, fostering a compassionate environment where emotions can be openly discussed.

### B. Seeking Understanding:

Create opportunities for your support network to learn about binge eating disorders. Share resources, attend educational events together, and engage in conversations that enhance their understanding of the challenges you may face.

## 5. Celebrating Progress Together:

### A. Milestone Recognition:

Celebrate milestones and achievements collectively. Acknowledging progress, no matter how small, reinforces positive behavior and creates a shared sense of accomplishment within the relationships that matter most.

### B. Joint Wellness Activities:

Engage in wellness activities together. Whether it's preparing healthy meals, participating in physical activities, or practicing mindfulness, shared experiences strengthen the bonds of support and contribute to the well-being of everyone involved.

## 6. Conflict Resolution and Growth:

### A. Constructive Conflict Resolution:

Learn and practice constructive conflict resolution. Disagreements are a natural part of relationships, but approaching conflicts respectfully, actively listening, and focusing on finding solutions contribute to overall relationship growth.

### B. Shared Learning and Growth:

View challenges as opportunities for shared learning and growth. Embrace the journey together, recognizing that the evolution of relationships is intertwined with the individual and collective pursuit of well-being.

# BUILDING NETWORKS FOR BINGE-FREE LIVING

In this section, we embark on a crucial exploration into the realm of supportive communities and resources—a cornerstone in the journey toward binge-free living. Engaging with communities and tapping into valuable resources enhances understanding, provides shared experiences, and offers a support network crucial for navigating the complexities of overcoming compulsive eating. Let's delve into comprehensive strategies for building connections and utilizing resources that empower your commitment to a balanced and mindful lifestyle.

## 1. Online Support Groups and Forums:

### A. Finding Reputable Platforms:

Explore reputable online support groups and forums focused on binge eating recovery. Platforms such as forums, social media groups, and dedicated websites offer a space for individuals to share experiences, seek advice, and provide mutual encouragement.

### B. Active Participation:

Engage actively within these communities. Share your journey, ask questions, and offer support to others. Active participation provides a sense of camaraderie and fosters a reciprocal exchange of insights and encouragement.

## 2. Local Support Networks:

### A. Community Centers and Events:

Investigate local community centers and events that focus on mental health and well-being. Attend workshops, seminars, or support group meetings where you can connect with individuals facing similar challenges and access local resources.

### B. Mental Health Professionals:

Seek guidance from mental health professionals who may facilitate or be aware of local support networks. Therapists, counselors, and nutritionists can provide valuable recommendations and connections within your community.

## 3. Educational Workshops and Webinars:

### A. Online Learning Platforms:

Explore online learning platforms that offer workshops and webinars on binge eating recovery. These resources often provide expert insights, practical tools, and a structured approach to understanding and overcoming compulsive eating.

### B. Attending Live Events:

Participate in live events, either in person or virtually, hosted by professionals in the field. These events can offer opportunities for direct interaction, Q&A sessions, and a deeper understanding of binge eating recovery strategies.

## 4. Seeking Professional Guidance:

### A. Nutritionists and Dietitians:

Consult with nutritionists or dietitians specializing in disordered eating. These professionals can offer personalized guidance on establishing a balanced and mindful approach to food, contributing to your overall journey toward binge-free living.

### B. Therapy and Counseling:

Consider therapy or counseling to address the emotional aspects of binge eating. Mental health professionals can provide tailored strategies, coping mechanisms, and a safe space for exploring the emotional roots of compulsive consumption.

## 5. Books and Literature on Binge Eating Recovery:

### A. Recommended Reading Lists:

Explore recommended reading lists focused on binge eating recovery. Books written by experts or individuals who have overcome similar challenges can provide valuable insights, practical advice, and a sense of empowerment.

### B. Book Clubs or Discussion Groups:

Join book clubs or discussion groups centered around binge eating recovery literature. Conversations with others who have read the same material can deepen your understanding and foster a sense of shared learning.

## 6. Utilizing Mobile Applications:

### A. Wellness Apps:

Explore wellness and mental health apps that cater to binge eating recovery. These apps often include features such as mood tracking, mindfulness exercises, and community forums, providing a convenient and accessible resource.

## B. Journaling and Goal-Tracking Apps:

Consider journaling or goal-tracking apps to document your journey and progress. These tools can offer a structured way to reflect on your experiences, set goals, and celebrate achievements.

## Conclusion

Cultivating healthy relationships and engaging with supportive communities are vital to your binge-free living journey. The connections you build have the power to uplift and sustain, forming a dynamic support network. This chapter is an exploration of the heart of these connections—an invitation to tap into a wealth of knowledge and experiences, enhancing your resilience and commitment to a life free from compulsive eating.

# CHAPTER 6

## MEAL PLANNING AND PREPARATION FOR BINGE-FREE LIVING

Welcome to Chapter 6, where we embark on a flavorful journey into the heart of meal planning and preparation—a pivotal chapter in the tapestry of binge-free living.

Beyond the mere act of sustenance, this exploration delves into cultivating a nourishing relationship with food. Join me as we uncover the strategies, flavors, and mindful practices that contribute to a balanced and satisfying meal approach, laying the foundation for a life free from compulsive consumption.

# HOW TO CREATE BALANCED AND DELICIOUS MEALS THAT MEET YOUR NEEDS

In this chapter, we embark on a culinary adventure, exploring the art of crafting balanced and delicious meals tailored to meet your physical and emotional needs. The journey toward binge-free living involves what you eat and how you engage with your meals. Let's unravel the principles of creating nourishing, satisfying, and mindful dishes that contribute to your well-being.

## 1. Understanding Balanced Nutrition:
### A. The Plate Method:
Adopt the plate method as a guide for balanced meals. Divide your plate into sections for

vegetables, lean proteins, whole grains, and healthy fats. This visual representation ensures a diverse and nutrient-rich combination in every meal.

**B. Nutrient Variety:**

Incorporate a variety of nutrients into your meals. Explore different fruits, vegetables, proteins, and grains to ensure your body receives a broad spectrum of essential vitamins and minerals.

**2. Mindful Meal Planning:**

**A. Preparing a Weekly Menu:**

Devote time to weekly meal planning. Outline your meals in advance, considering a mix of flavors and textures. Planning helps you make intentional choices, reducing the likelihood of impulsive eating.

**B. Creating Balanced Combinations:**

Pair macronutrients thoughtfully. Combine carbohydrates, proteins, and fats to create a satisfying and well-rounded meal. This balance contributes to sustained energy levels and satiety.

## 3. Portion Control and Moderation:

### A. Mindful Portions:

Practice mindful portion control. Be attuned to hunger and fullness cues, serving portions that align with your body's needs. Avoid restrictive practices, aiming for moderation and a healthy relationship with food.

### B. Balanced Snacking:

Incorporate balanced snacks between meals. Opt for nutrient-dense options like yogurt with fruit or a handful of nuts to maintain energy levels and prevent overindulgence during main meals.

## 4. Culinary Creativity:

### A. Exploring Flavors and Textures:

Explore a variety of flavors and textures in your meals. Experiment with herbs, spices, and different cooking methods to enhance the sensory experience of eating, making each meal a delightful journey for the palate.

### B. Colorful and Vibrant Plates:

Craft visually appealing plates by incorporating a spectrum of colors. Vibrant fruits and vegetables provide essential nutrients and make your meals visually enticing.

## 5. Listening to Cravings Mindfully:

### A. Differentiating Hunger and Cravings:

Practice mindful eating by distinguishing between true hunger and emotional cravings. Before reaching for a snack, pause and assess whether your body is genuinely hungry or if there's an emotional trigger.

### B. Satisfying Cravings Healthily:

If cravings arise, find healthy alternatives that satisfy your desires. For example, if you crave something sweet, choose a piece of fruit or a small serving of dark chocolate to balance indulgence with nutritional value.

## 6. Incorporating Diverse Cuisine:

### A. Global Culinary Exploration:

Broaden your culinary horizons by exploring diverse cuisines. Incorporate ingredients and recipes from different cultures, introducing a rich tapestry of flavors and expanding your repertoire of balanced and delicious meals.

### B. Adapting Recipes to Your Needs:

Modify recipes to meet your nutritional needs. Substitute ingredients, adjust portions, and experiment with cooking techniques to tailor meals to your preferences and dietary requirements.

# HOW TO PRACTICE MINDFUL EATING AND SAVOR YOUR FOOD

In this section, we embark on a mindful exploration into the practice of eating—an art that goes beyond nourishment to embrace the full sensory experience of savoring each bite. Mindful eating is a transformative approach that contributes to binge-free living by fostering a deeper connection with consuming food. Let's unravel the principles and techniques that lead to a more conscious, satisfying, and joyful relationship with the nourishment we provide our bodies.

## 1. Cultivating Present-Moment Awareness:

### A. Engaging the Senses:

Initiate your mindful eating journey by engaging your senses. Notice the colors, textures, and aromas of your food. Be present in the moment, appreciating the sensory richness that each meal brings.

### B. Eliminating Distractions:

Create a dedicated eating environment by minimizing distractions. Turn off electronic devices, step away from work, and focus solely on eating. This intentional space enhances your ability to savor and enjoy your food.

## 2. Tuning into Hunger and Fullness:

### A. Listening to Body Signals:

Practice tuning into your body's signals of hunger and fullness. Eat when you're hungry, and pause to assess your satisfaction level throughout the meal. Mindful eating encourages a more intuitive and attuned approach to nourishment.

**B. Recognizing Emotional Cues:**

Distinguish between physical hunger and emotional cues. Before reaching for food, assess whether your body genuinely requires sustenance or if underlying emotional triggers influence your desire to eat.

**3. Slow and Deliberate Eating:**

**A. Chewing Mindfully:**

Chew your food slowly and deliberately. Mindful chewing not only aids digestion but allows you to savor the flavors and textures of each bite. Counting your chews can be a simple practice to cultivate this awareness.

### B. Setting Down Utensils:

Between bites, set down your utensils. This intentional pause encourages you to focus on chewing and savoring rather than rushing through the meal. It promotes a rhythm of eating that aligns with your body's natural signals.

## 4. Expressing Gratitude:

### A. Reflecting on Food Origins:

Before eating, take a moment to reflect on the journey of your food—from its origins to your plate. Express gratitude for its nourishment and the efforts involved in its production and preparation.

### B. Mindful Reflection Post-Meal:

After completing your meal, reflect mindfully on the experience. Notice how your body feels, any emotions that arise, and your overall satisfaction. This reflective practice enhances your awareness of the connections between food and well-being.

## 5. Mindful Portioning:

### A. Serving Mindful Portions:

When serving your food, do so with mindfulness. Consider your hunger level, and serve portions that align with your body's needs. Avoid overfilling your plate, allowing space for mindful eating practices.

### B. Appreciating Moderation:

Embrace the concept of moderation. Mindful eating is not about restriction but savoring and appreciating the flavors within reasonable portions. This practice supports a balanced and sustainable approach to eating.

## 6. Connecting with Your Food:

### A. Farm-to-Table Awareness:

Enhance your connection with food by understanding its source. Explore local and seasonal produce, support farmers' markets, and consider the journey of your food from its origin to your plate. This awareness deepens your appreciation for the nourishment you receive.

**B. Mindful Cooking Practices:**

Extend mindfulness to the cooking process. Engage in the preparation of your meals with attention and intention. Cooking becomes a meditative practice, aligning your energy with the creation of nourishing dishes.

## Conclusion

Creating balanced meals is an art, an expression of self-care central to binge-free living. The kitchen is a canvas for mindful nourishment—an invitation to savor, celebrate culinary creativity, and cultivate joy. Likewise, mindful eating is a transformative journey, a celebration of each bite and a communion with your food. It's about more than what you eat—it's an invitation to savor the present moment, find joy in culinary exploration, and foster a profound connection between body, mind, and nourishment. Together, they form a unique tapestry, weaving the threads of culinary harmony and mindful joy into your journey toward lasting well-being.

# CHAPTER 7

# SETTING AND ACHIEVING GOALS FOR BINGE-FREE LIVING

Welcome to Chapter 7, A Compass for your journey toward empowerment—where we delve into the transformative process of setting and achieving goals for binge-free living. This chapter navigates the landscape of aspirations, milestones, and personal triumphs. Join me in unlocking the power of intentional goal-setting as we chart a course toward a life free from compulsive consumption, celebrating every achievement.

# HOW TO ESTABLISH REALISTIC AND MEANINGFUL MILESTONES

In this part, we set milestones—an integral aspect of the journey toward binge-free living. Realistic and meaningful milestones act as guideposts, illuminating the path of progress and providing tangible markers of success. Let's unravel the principles and strategies for establishing achievable and meaningful milestones, fostering a sense of empowerment and accomplishment.

## 1. Reflecting on Your Journey:

### A. Acknowledging Starting Points:

Begin by acknowledging your starting point in the journey toward binge-free living. Reflect on your current habits, challenges, and successes. This self-awareness forms the foundation for establishing milestones that align with your unique path.

### B. Identifying Triggers and Patterns:

Identify triggers and patterns associated with binge eating. Understanding the root causes of compulsive consumption allows you to set milestones that address specific challenges, creating a more targeted and effective approach.

## 2. Setting Specific and Attainable Goals:

### A. Defining Clear Objectives:

Set specific and clear objectives for your binge-free living journey. Instead of vague goals, such as "eat healthier," define specific actions, such as "incorporate one extra serving of vegetables into each meal." Clarity enhances your ability to measure progress.

**B. Gradual Progression:**

Establish attainable milestones that reflect gradual progression. Break down large goals into smaller, manageable steps. This approach makes the journey more manageable and celebrates achievements along the way.

## 3. Aligning Goals with Core Values:

**A. Connecting with Personal Values:**

Align your milestones with your core values. Consider how achieving each goal contributes to your overall well-being and aligns with the values that are important to you. Connecting goals to deeper motivations enhances their significance.

**B. Ensuring Personal Relevance:**

Ensure that each milestone holds personal relevance. Tailor goals to your individual needs and aspirations, recognizing that meaningful milestones resonate with your unique journey and foster a sense of purpose.

## 4. Incorporating Behavioral Changes:

### A. Identifying Behavioral Shifts:

Delineate specific behavioral changes associated with each milestone. Whether it's developing healthier coping mechanisms, practicing mindfulness, or cultivating positive eating habits, clearly articulate the behavioral shifts you aim to achieve.

### B. Embracing Positive Habits:

Frame milestones as opportunities to embrace positive habits. Focus on cultivating behaviors contributing to binge-free living, reinforcing that each milestone is a step toward building a sustainable and healthy lifestyle.

## 5. Measuring Progress Thoughtfully:

**A. Establishing Measurable Metrics:**

Identify measurable metrics for each milestone. Whether tracking the frequency of binge episodes, monitoring emotional well-being, or noting changes in eating patterns, establish clear criteria to gauge progress.

**B. Celebrating Small Wins:**

Celebrate small wins along the way. Acknowledge and appreciate even the incremental achievements as they contribute to the overall momentum of your journey. Cultivating a positive mindset reinforces your commitment to the process.

**6. Adapting Goals to Evolving Circumstances:**

**A. Flexibility in Goal-Setting:**

Recognize the need for flexibility in goal-setting. Life is dynamic, and circumstances may change.

Allow for adjustments to your milestones, ensuring they remain relevant to your evolving needs and challenges.

**B. Learning from Setbacks:**

View setbacks as learning opportunities. If you encounter challenges in achieving a milestone, assess the factors contributing to the setback and use the insights gained to refine your approach. Every obstacle is a stepping stone to growth.

# HOW TO CELEBRATE YOUR SUCCESSES AND LEARN FROM YOUR CHALLENGES

In this part, we embark on a vital aspect of the binge-free living journey—acknowledging successes and embracing challenges as opportunities for growth. Celebrating achievements and learning from setbacks are integral to cultivating resilience, self-compassion, and a sustainable path toward a life free from compulsive eating. Let's explore strategies and mindful practices that empower you to honor your successes and gracefully navigate challenges.

## 1. Cultivating a Positive Mindset:

### A. Recognizing Achievements:

Cultivate a positive mindset by recognizing and celebrating your achievements. Acknowledge even the smallest successes, whether it's a day without binge eating or a positive shift in your mindset. This practice reinforces a sense of accomplishment.

### B. Shifting Focus to Positivity:

Shift your focus from perceived failures to positive outcomes. When faced with challenges, consciously redirect your attention to the progress you've made and the strengths you've demonstrated. Positivity fuels motivation and resilience.

## 2. Establishing Rituals of Celebration:

### A. Personalized Milestone Celebrations:

Establish personalized rituals to celebrate milestones. Whether it's treating yourself to a favorite activity, enjoying a nourishing meal, or practicing self-care, create rituals that honor your journey and the achievements you've reached.

### B. Involve Supportive Others:

Share your successes with supportive individuals in your life. Celebrating with friends, family, or members of your support network enhances the joy of success and strengthens your connections.

## 3. Reflecting on Growth:

### A. Journaling Achievements:

Maintain a success journal to document and reflect on your achievements. Write down the milestones you've reached, the challenges you've overcome, and the personal growth you've experienced. Journaling reinforces a positive narrative.

### B. Gratitude Practice:

Incorporate a gratitude practice into your celebration rituals. Express gratitude for the progress you've made, the lessons learned from challenges, and the support you've received. Gratitude enhances your overall well-being.

## 4. Learning from Setbacks:

### A. Embracing a Growth Mindset:

Approach challenges with a growth mindset. View setbacks as opportunities for learning and growth rather than as failures. Embracing a growth mindset fosters resilience and encourages a proactive approach to overcoming obstacles.

### B. Analyzing Triggering Factors:

When facing challenges, analyze triggering factors without self-judgment. Identify the circumstances, emotions, or behaviors that contributed to the setback. This awareness provides valuable insights for refining your strategies moving forward.

### 5. Seeking Support and Guidance:

### A. Turning to Your Support Network:

Lean on your support network during challenging times. Share your experiences, seek advice, and draw strength from the understanding and encouragement of those who accompany you.

### B. Professional Guidance:

Consider seeking professional guidance to navigate challenges effectively. Therapists, counselors, or nutritionists specializing in binge eating recovery can offer valuable insights, coping strategies, and personalized support.

## 6. Adjusting and Reframing Goals:

### A. Flexibility in Goal Adjustment:

Maintain flexibility in adjusting goals based on your evolving needs and circumstances. If a particular goal becomes challenging, consider modifying it to align with your current situation, ensuring it remains realistic and attainable.

### B. Reframing Challenges as Opportunities:

Reframe challenges as opportunities for self-discovery and growth. Each obstacle faced is a chance to refine your approach, strengthen your coping mechanisms, and deepen your understanding of yourself and your journey.

### **<u>Conclusion</u>**

Establishing realistic milestones is an empowering investment in your journey toward binge-free living—a declaration of resilience and dedication. Simultaneously, celebrating successes and learning from challenges is a dynamic process, essential to your transformative journey. This exploration invites you to set goals aligned with your core, fostering a path defined by mindful choices. Embrace the richness of experiences, recognizing every celebration and challenge as an opportunity for profound self-discovery and sustainable growth.

# CHAPTER 8

# SEEKING PROFESSIONAL GUIDANCE FOR BINGE EATING

Step into Chapter 8, a compass for those seeking the expertise of professionals in their journey toward overcoming binge eating. In this chapter, we unravel the significance of professional guidance—a pivotal element beyond personal efforts. Join me as we explore the avenues of support offered by healthcare professionals, therapists, and counselors, delving into how their insights can illuminate the path to a life free from the confines of compulsive consumption.

# HOW TO WORK WITH HEALTHCARE PROFESSIONALS TO ADDRESS YOUR BINGE EATING

How to Work with Healthcare Professionals to Address Your Binge Eating: A Collaborative Approach to Wellness

In this section, we delve into the collaborative journey of seeking guidance from healthcare professionals to address binge eating—a crucial step toward comprehensive wellness. Working with healthcare professionals, including physicians, nutritionists, and other specialists, enhances your understanding of the complexities involved in binge eating and provides tailored strategies for effective intervention. Let's explore the principles and strategies for establishing a constructive partnership with healthcare professionals on your path to a life free from compulsive consumption.

## 1. Initiating the Conversation:

### A. Open and Honest Communication:

Initiate the conversation with healthcare professionals through open and honest communication. Share your experiences, concerns, and goals related to binge eating. A comprehensive overview enables professionals to tailor their guidance to your unique needs.

### B. Seeking Non-Judgmental Support:

Look for healthcare professionals who offer non-judgmental support. A compassionate and understanding approach creates a safe space for discussing sensitive topics related to binge eating, fostering a collaborative and trusting relationship.

## 2. Seeking a Comprehensive Assessment:

### A. Medical Evaluation:

Undergo a comprehensive medical evaluation to identify any underlying health issues related to binge eating. Medical professionals can assess physical health, address nutritional imbalances, and rule out potential medical contributors to the behavior.

### B. Nutritional Assessment:

Collaborate with nutritionists for a thorough nutritional assessment. Understanding your dietary habits, nutrient intake, and potential deficiencies informs the development of personalized nutritional strategies to support your well-being.

## 3. Developing a Personalized Treatment Plan:

### A. Individualized Approach:

Work with healthcare professionals to develop an individualized treatment plan. Tailoring strategies to your specific needs, preferences, and challenges enhances the effectiveness of interventions and promotes long-term success.

**B. Multidisciplinary Collaboration:**

Engage in multidisciplinary collaboration. Professionals from various fields, such as psychology, nutrition, and psychiatry, can collaborate to address different aspects of binge eating, providing a holistic and comprehensive approach to treatment.

## 4. Exploring Therapeutic Interventions:

### A. Cognitive-Behavioral Therapy (CBT):

Consider Cognitive-Behavioral Therapy (CBT) as a therapeutic intervention. CBT is an evidence-based approach that addresses distorted thought patterns and behaviors associated with binge eating, promoting healthier coping mechanisms.

**B. Dialectical Behavior Therapy (DBT):**
Explore Dialectical Behavior Therapy (DBT) for emotion regulation and mindfulness skills. DBT can be beneficial in managing emotional triggers and developing a more balanced and mindful approach to eating.

## 5. Medication Management:

### A. Consultation with Psychiatrists:
Consider consultation with psychiatrists for medication management. In some instances, medications may be prescribed to you to address underlying mental health conditions contributing to binge eating, such as depression or anxiety.

### B. Monitoring Medication Effects:
Maintain open communication with healthcare professionals regarding the effects of prescribed

medications. Regular monitoring ensures adjustments can be made as needed, optimizing the therapeutic benefits of medication.

## 6. Regular Follow-Up Sessions:

### A. Accountability and Progress Tracking:

Participate in regular follow-up sessions with healthcare professionals. These sessions provide opportunities for accountability, progress tracking, and adjustments to the treatment plan based on your evolving needs and experiences.

### B. Addressing Challenges and Setbacks:

Use follow-up sessions to address challenges and setbacks. Discussing difficulties openly with healthcare professionals allows for collaborative problem-solving and ensures timely adjustments to the treatment plan.

# HOW TO BENEFIT FROM THERAPY AND COUNSELING FOR BINGE EATING

In this section, we delve into the transformative power of therapy and counseling as essential tools for overcoming binge eating. Seeking therapeutic support is a proactive and empowering step toward lasting recovery. Let's explore the comprehensive strategies and insights that therapy and counseling can offer, providing a roadmap for understanding, managing, and ultimately breaking free from the cycle of compulsive consumption.

**1. Embracing Individualized Counseling:**

**A. Personalized Therapeutic Relationships:**

Embark on a journey of individualized counseling. Establishing a therapeutic relationship with a counselor or therapist provides a safe and confidential space to explore the unique aspects of your experience with binge eating.

**B. Tailoring Approaches to Your Needs:**

Work with your therapist to tailor therapeutic approaches to your specific needs. Whether through cognitive-behavioral therapy (CBT), dialectical behavior therapy (DBT), or other evidence-based modalities, customization ensures interventions align with your goals and challenges.

## 2. Unraveling the Roots of Binge Eating:

### A. Exploring Emotional Triggers:

Therapy provides a platform to explore the emotional roots of binge eating. Dive into the underlying triggers, addressing past experiences, emotions, or traumas that contribute to the development and persistence of compulsive consumption.

**B. Identifying Negative Thought Patterns:** Collaborate with your therapist to identify negative thought patterns associated with binge eating. Cognitive exploration allows for recognizing and restructuring distorted beliefs, fostering healthier perceptions of self and food.

## 3. Developing Coping Mechanisms:

**A. Learning Adaptive Coping Skills:** Therapy equips you with adaptive coping skills. Through sessions, you'll acquire practical tools to manage stress, anxiety, and emotional challenges without resorting to binge eating. These skills empower you to navigate life's complexities more effectively.

**B. Mindfulness and Emotional Regulation:**
Explore mindfulness techniques and emotional regulation strategies. Therapy guides you in cultivating mindfulness, enabling you to stay present with your emotions and respond to them in a balanced and constructive manner.

**4. Establishing a Supportive Therapeutic Alliance:**

**A. Building Trust and Connection:**
Establish a supportive therapeutic alliance with your counselor. Building trust and connection is foundational for effective therapy, creating a space where you feel heard, understood, and supported in your journey toward recovery.

**B. Open Communication and Feedback:**
Cultivate open communication and provide feedback during therapy. Your active involvement ensures the therapeutic process

remains collaborative, allowing for adjustments to approaches and interventions based on your evolving needs.

## 5. Addressing Co-occurring Mental Health Conditions:

### A. Integrated Mental Health Support:

Therapy addresses co-occurring mental health conditions. If you're experiencing conditions such as depression, anxiety, or trauma alongside binge eating, integrated mental health support helps address these interconnected challenges.

### B. Medication Consultation:

Consider consultation with a psychiatrist for medication management if necessary. Collaborative care between therapists and psychiatrists ensures a comprehensive approach, addressing your well-being's psychological and physiological aspects.

## 6. Incorporating Family and Group Therapy:

### A. Involving Support Systems:

Family therapy offers a platform to involve your support system. Engaging family members in therapy can enhance understanding, improve communication, and foster a more supportive environment for your recovery.

### B. Group Therapy Dynamics:

Explore the dynamics of group therapy. Participating in group sessions provides a sense of community, shared experiences, and mutual support, creating a space where individuals can learn from one another and foster collective growth.

## Conclusion

Working with healthcare professionals and embracing therapy are courageous steps toward overcoming binge eating. Seeking guidance is a proactive choice for comprehensive well-being—a collaborative exploration inviting you to embrace support and expertise. This transformative journey paves the way for a life marked by mindfulness, balance, resilience, and freedom from the constraints of compulsive consumption.

# CHAPTER 9

# MAINTAINING BINGE-FREE LIVING IN THE LONG TERM

Step into Chapter 9, a guide to the art of sustained freedom—where we explore the strategies, mindset, and practices essential for maintaining binge-free living in the long term. This chapter is a compass for those who have embarked on the transformative journey of overcoming compulsive consumption, providing insights into the enduring principles that contribute to lasting liberation. Join me as we unravel the keys to a life marked by balance, resilience, and the enduring victory over the shadows of binge eating.

# HOW TO DEVELOP STRATEGIES FOR PREVENTING AND OVERCOMING RELAPSES

In this crucial section, we delve into the art of fortification—crafting robust strategies to prevent and overcome relapses on your journey to lasting binge-free living. Relapses are part of the recovery process, but armed with effective tools and a resilient mindset, you can navigate these challenges and emerge stronger. Let's explore comprehensive strategies that act as safeguards and empower you to overcome setbacks and continue the path to sustained well-being.

## 1. Understanding Triggers and Warning Signs:

### A. Self-Reflection and Awareness:

Initiate a process of self-reflection to identify triggers and warning signs leading to binge eating. Heightened self-awareness allows you to recognize potential pitfalls early on, empowering you to implement preventive strategies proactively.

### B. Journaling and Tracking:

Maintain a relapse prevention journal to track emotions, situations, or thought patterns that precede relapses. This documented insight becomes a valuable resource for anticipating challenges and refining prevention strategies.

## 2. Building a Resilient Mindset:

### A. Embracing a Growth Mindset:

Cultivate a growth mindset that views relapses as opportunities for learning and growth rather than failures. Embracing setbacks with resilience allows you to extract valuable lessons and reinforces your commitment to the journey.

**B. Positive Affirmations and Visualization:** Incorporate positive affirmations and visualization techniques to bolster your mental resilience. Envisioning success and reinforcing positive beliefs about your ability to overcome challenges contribute to a mindset geared for lasting recovery.

### 3. Establishing a Supportive Network:

### A. Strengthening Support Systems:

Nurture and strengthen your support network. Communicate openly with friends, family, or support groups about your journey, relapse triggers, and the support you find most beneficial. A robust support system acts as a crucial anchor during challenging times.

**B. Emergency Contacts and Crisis Plans:**
Develop a list of emergency contacts and a crisis plan. Share this plan with trusted individuals who can offer immediate support during vulnerable moments. Having a structured response strategy enhances your ability to navigate crises effectively.

**4. Mindful Coping Strategies:**

**A. Mindfulness and Grounding Techniques:**
Integrate mindfulness and grounding techniques into your daily routine. Mindful practices, such as deep breathing, meditation, or grounding exercises, serve as powerful tools to redirect your focus and manage stressors that may lead to relapse.

**B. Engaging in Healthy Distractions:**

Identify and engage in healthy distractions when cravings arise. Redirecting your attention to activities you enjoy—reading, exercising, or pursuing a hobby—provides an alternative outlet for managing emotional triggers.

## 5. Developing a Personalized Relapse Prevention Plan:

**A. Collaborating with Professionals:**

Collaborate with healthcare professionals and therapists to create a personalized relapse prevention plan. Professionals can offer tailored strategies, coping mechanisms, and interventions based on your unique triggers and challenges.

**B. Regular Review and Adjustment:**

Regularly review and adjust your prevention plan. As you evolve in your recovery, the effectiveness of certain strategies may change. A dynamic and evolving plan ensures it remains relevant and adaptive to your current needs.

## 6. Learning from Relapses:

### A. Analyzing Relapse Triggers:

After a relapse, analyze the triggers and circumstances without self-judgment. Understanding the factors contributing to the relapse provides insights for refining your prevention strategies and bolstering your resilience.

### B. Seeking Professional Guidance:

If relapses become recurrent, consider seeking additional professional guidance. Therapists, counselors, or support groups specializing in relapse prevention can offer targeted interventions and support to address persistent challenges.

# HOW TO CREATE A PERSONALIZED MAINTENANCE PLAN THAT WORKS FOR YOU

This section explores the art of customization—a guide to crafting a personalized maintenance plan that aligns seamlessly with your unique needs, preferences, and aspirations. As you traverse the path to sustained binge-free living, a tailored maintenance plan becomes your compass, providing structure, accountability, and a roadmap for lasting well-being. Let's delve into the comprehensive strategies and considerations for developing a plan that works for you and empowers you on your continued journey to freedom from compulsive consumption.

**1. Reflecting on Your Progress:**

**A. Celebrating Achievements:**

Begin by celebrating your achievements and milestones. Reflect on your progress in your binge-free living journey, acknowledging small victories and significant triumphs. Positive reinforcement sets the stage for a constructive maintenance plan.

**B. Identifying Persistent Challenges:**

Conduct a candid assessment of persistent challenges. Identify areas where you may encounter difficulties and consider the lessons learned from setbacks. This self-awareness informs the customization of your maintenance plan to address potential hurdles.

**2. Tailoring Strategies to Your Lifestyle:**

**A. Aligning with Your Routine:**

Craft strategies that seamlessly align with your daily routine. Consider your work schedule, social activities, and personal preferences when designing your maintenance plan. A plan integrated into your lifestyle enhances its sustainability.

**B. Flexibility and Adaptability:**

Prioritize flexibility and adaptability. Recognize that life is dynamic, and your maintenance plan should accommodate changes in circumstances. A flexible approach allows you to adjust strategies without compromising the overall integrity of your plan.

## 3. Building Sustainable Habits:

### A. Gradual Incorporation of Habits:

Incorporate sustainable habits gradually. Rather than overwhelming yourself with numerous changes, introduce one or two new habits at a time. This gradual approach promotes long-term adherence and prevents burnout.

### B. Consistency over Intensity:

Emphasize consistency over intensity. Aim for sustainable, small changes that become integral to daily life. Consistent habits contribute to the stability and longevity of your maintenance plan.

## 4. Utilizing Support Systems:

### A. Engaging with Your Support Network:

Integrate your support network into your maintenance plan. Share your goals and strategies with friends, family, or support groups, fostering a collaborative environment that enhances accountability and encouragement.

### B. Professional Check-Ins:

Consider scheduling regular check-ins with healthcare professionals or therapists. Professional guidance provides an external perspective, offers valuable insights, and ensures your maintenance plan aligns with your evolving needs.

## 5. Monitoring and Evaluation:

### A. Establishing Tracking Mechanisms:

Implement tracking mechanisms to monitor your progress. Whether through journaling, apps, or other tools, regularly assess how well your maintenance plan aligns with your goals and make adjustments as needed.

### B. Periodic Evaluations:

Conduct periodic evaluations of your maintenance plan. Set specific intervals for reviewing its effectiveness, identifying areas for improvement, and refining strategies to enhance overall efficacy.

## 6. Addressing Emotional Well-Being:

### A. Emotional Check-Ins:

Incorporate emotional check-ins into your maintenance routine. Regularly assess your emotional well-being, addressing any stressors or emotional triggers that may impact your adherence to the plan. Emotional awareness enhances resilience.

### B. Revisiting Coping Mechanisms:

Revisit and reinforce coping mechanisms. Ensure that your maintenance plan includes strategies for managing stress, anxiety, and other emotions effectively, fortifying your ability to navigate challenging moments.

## 7. Setting Realistic Milestones:

### A. Realistic and Attainable Goals:

Establish realistic and attainable milestones within your maintenance plan. Goals should reflect your ongoing growth and progress, providing a sense of accomplishment while maintaining a sustainable pace.

**B. Celebrating Milestones:**

Celebrate milestones with intention. Acknowledge and celebrate your achievements, reinforcing the positive behaviors and habits cultivated through your maintenance plan. Celebrations contribute to a positive feedback loop of motivation.

## Conclusion

Developing strategies for relapse prevention is an integral part of the journey toward lasting recovery—a dynamic process embracing growth, not failure. Equipping yourself with resilience and self-awareness transforms setbacks into stepping stones. Simultaneously, creating a personalized maintenance plan is an art of self-discovery and empowerment—an evolving reflection of your journey. This exploration invites you to embrace the freedom and agency that customization offers, ensuring your plan is a living testament to your commitment to sustained binge-free living.

# CHAPTER 10

## HOLISTIC SELF-CARE FOR BINGE-FREE LIVING

Welcome to Chapter 10, a sanctuary of self-care—a holistic exploration that goes beyond the surface and embraces the interconnected well-being of your mind, body, and spirit. In this chapter, we embark on a journey of nurturing the essence of who you are, weaving together practices that cultivate balance, joy, and a profound sense of self. Join me as we delve into the tapestry of holistic self-care, illuminating pathways toward a life marked by wellness, resilience, and enduring freedom from the shadows of binge eating.

# WHY SELF-CARE IS ESSENTIAL FOR YOUR HEALTH AND HAPPINESS

In the hustle and bustle of daily life, self-care emerges as a beacon of well-being—a deliberate and compassionate act that transcends mere indulgence. This chapter explores the profound reasons why self-care is a luxury and an essential cornerstone for cultivating enduring health and happiness. Let's unravel the layers of this holistic perspective, delving into the intricate interplay between self-care, mental resilience, physical vitality, and the pursuit of genuine happiness.

## 1. Nurturing Mental Resilience:

**A. Stress Reduction and Coping Mechanisms:**

Self-care serves as a powerful tool for nurturing mental resilience. Engaging in activities that bring joy, relaxation, and peace helps reduce stress. Furthermore, it provides an opportunity to develop and reinforce effective coping mechanisms for life's inevitable challenges.

**B. Emotional Regulation and Well-Being:**

Self-care improves emotional regulation, fostering a more balanced and positive emotional state. Self-care becomes a proactive strategy for maintaining overall emotional well-being when consistently integrated into your routine.

**2. Physical Vitality and Wellness:**

**A. Rest and Recovery:**

Prioritizing rest and recovery is an integral aspect of self-care. Whether through sufficient sleep, relaxation techniques, or mindful pauses during the day, self-care supports the body's natural rejuvenation processes, enhancing physical vitality and resilience.

**B. Nutrition and Nourishment:**

Self-care extends to mindful nutrition and nourishment. By making conscious choices about the food you consume, you support your physical health and cultivate a deeper connection to the body and its needs.

**3. Cultivating a Positive Mindset:**

**A. Self-Compassion and Positive Affirmations:**

Self-care is a pathway to cultivating self-compassion. Embracing self-kindness and positive affirmations nurtures a positive mindset, fostering a more optimistic and resilient outlook.

B. Mindfulness and Present-Moment Awareness: Incorporating mindfulness practices into self-care routines promotes present-moment awareness. Being fully present allows you to savor life's experiences, reduce anxiety about the future, and break free from the hold of past regrets.

## 4. Building a Foundation for Happiness:

### A. Aligning with Personal Values:

Self-care aligns with the pursuit of happiness by allowing you to align your actions with your values. Engaging in activities that resonate with your core values creates a sense of purpose and fulfillment.

### B. Joyful Pursuits and Leisure:

Including joyful pursuits and leisure in your self-care routine contributes directly to happiness. Whether it's hobbies, creative expressions, or simply taking time for activities that bring joy, these moments become the building blocks of a fulfilling life.

## 5. Strengthening Relationships:

### A. Boundary Setting and Healthy Relationships:

Self-care involves setting boundaries, a crucial component in maintaining healthy relationships. By prioritizing your well-being, you create space for meaningful connections based on mutual respect and understanding.

### B. Emotional Availability:

When you practice self-care, you enhance your emotional availability in relationships. A well-nurtured individual is better equipped to offer genuine support, empathy, and connection to others.

## 6. Preventing Burnout and Overwhelm:

### A. Proactive Stress Management:

Regular self-care serves as a preventive measure against burnout and overwhelm. Instead of waiting until stress reaches a critical point, consistent self-care routines allow for proactive stress management, ensuring a more sustainable and balanced lifestyle.

### B. Recognizing Signs of Overwhelm:

Self-care involves being attuned to your needs and recognizing signs of being overwhelmed. By developing this awareness, you can implement timely interventions and adjustments, preventing escalating stress to unmanageable levels.

# HOW TO INCORPORATE HOLISTIC WELLNESS PRACTICES INTO YOUR DAILY LIFE

In this transformative part, we delve into the art of integration—crafting a lifestyle that embraces holistic wellness practices as integral elements of your daily routine. Holistic wellness extends beyond physical health, encompassing mental clarity, emotional balance, and spiritual nourishment.

Join me as we explore comprehensive strategies and actionable steps for seamlessly infusing holistic practices into the fabric of your daily life, fostering enduring well-being.

**1. Morning Rituals for Mindful Beginnings:**

**A. Mindful Wake-Up Routine:**

Start your day with intention and mindfulness. Incorporate a mindful wake-up routine that may include gentle stretching, deep breathing, or moments of gratitude. This sets a positive tone for the day ahead.

**B. Nourishing Breakfast Ritual:**

Make breakfast a nourishing ritual. Choose nutrient-dense foods and savor your meal mindfully. This not only supports physical well-being but also establishes a mindful approach to eating.

**2. Mindfulness Throughout the Day:**

**A. Mini Meditation Breaks:**

Integrate mini-meditation breaks into your day. Take a few minutes to pause, breathe deeply, and center yourself. These moments of mindfulness can enhance focus, reduce stress, and foster emotional balance.

## B. Mindful Movement Practices:

Incorporate mindful movement practices such as yoga or tai chi. These activities contribute to physical fitness and promote mental clarity and emotional well-being.

## 3. Cultivating Emotional Resilience:

### A. Journaling for Emotional Expression:

Allocate time for journaling to express and process your emotions. This reflective practice provides a constructive outlet for emotional expression and self-discovery.

### B. Gratitude Practice:

Cultivate a gratitude practice. Regularly reflect on the positive aspects of your life, fostering a mindset of appreciation and resilience in the face of challenges.

## 4. Holistic Nutrition for Nourishment:

### A. Mindful Eating Habits:

Practice mindful eating habits. Pay attention to the flavors, textures, and sensations of your food. This mindful approach enhances the nutritional experience and supports digestive well-being.

### B. Hydration Rituals:

Establish hydration rituals. Ensure you consistently consume adequate water throughout the day, promoting optimal bodily functions and overall vitality.

## 5. Movement as a Daily Ritual:

### A. Incorporating Joyful Movement:

Make movement a joyful daily ritual. Engage in activities you love, whether a nature walk, dance, or any exercise that brings pleasure. Movement becomes a celebration of vitality.

**B. Balancing Work and Rest:**

Strive for a balance between activity and rest. Recognize the importance of both movement and adequate rest in maintaining overall well-being.

## 6. Evening Practices for Tranquil Endings:

**A. Relaxing Evening Routine:**

Create a relaxing evening routine. Include activities that promote relaxation, such as reading, gentle stretching, or a calming meditation. This prepares your body and mind for restful sleep.

**B. Digital Detox Before Bed:**

Implement a digital detox before bedtime. Limit screen time to promote quality sleep, allowing your mind to unwind and rejuvenate.

## 7. Connecting with Nature:

### A. Outdoor Activities:

Spend time in nature. Whether it's a walk in the park, gardening, or simply sitting outdoors, connecting with nature enhances mental well-being and provides a sense of tranquility.

### B. Grounding Practices:

Practice grounding techniques, such as walking barefoot on natural surfaces. Grounding fosters a connection with the earth and promotes a sense of balance.

## 8. Spiritual Exploration and Connection:

### A. Meditation and Contemplation:

Incorporate meditation or contemplative practices into your routine. These moments of spiritual connection contribute to a sense of purpose and inner harmony.

### B. Exploring Spiritual Traditions:

Explore spiritual traditions that resonate with you. This may involve reading sacred texts, attending spiritual gatherings, or engaging in practices that align with your beliefs.

## **Conclusion**

Self-care is the compass guiding you toward health and happiness—an investment, not selfishness. This journey invites you to unlock enduring health, resilience, and genuine happiness through profound self-care. Simultaneously, holistic wellness practices are threads woven into your daily tapestry.

As we navigate together, remember that this intentional exploration fosters enduring balance and vitality—a gradual journey honoring the interconnectedness of mind, body, and spirit.

# CHAPTER 11

# MINDFUL REFLECTION AND JOURNALING FOR BINGE-FREE LIVING

Step into Chapter 11, a sanctuary of self-discovery—an exploration of mindful reflection and journaling as transformative tools on your journey to lasting freedom from compulsive consumption.

In this chapter, we embark on a guided odyssey into your thoughts, emotions, and aspirations, using the power of mindful reflection and journaling to illuminate the path toward a more profound understanding of your relationship with food and self. Join me as we delve into the art of introspection, unlocking the doors to insights, healing, and enduring liberation from the shadows of binge eating.

# HOW TO USE JOURNALING AS A TOOL FOR SELF-DISCOVERY AND HEALING

In this transformative exploration, we delve into the profound practice of journaling—a tool for self-discovery, reflection, and healing on the journey to lasting freedom from compulsive consumption.

Journaling is more than ink on paper; it is a conduit for expressing your innermost thoughts, navigating emotions, and unveiling the narratives that shape your relationship with food and self.

Let's embark on a guided journey into the art of journaling, unraveling the comprehensive ways in which it becomes a potent tool for self-exploration and empowerment.

## 1. Establishing a Safe and Sacred Space:

### A. Choosing a Journal:

Select a journal that resonates with you. Whether it's a blank notebook, a digital platform, or a guided journal, choose a format that feels like a safe and sacred space for your thoughts and reflections.

### B. Creating a Ritual:

Establish a journaling ritual. Choose a consistent time and place for your journaling practice, creating a ritual that signals to your mind the importance and sacredness of this introspective journey.

## 2. Expressing Your Authentic Voice:

### A. Honesty and Authenticity:

Cultivate honesty and authenticity in your writing. Use your journal as a space where you can express your true thoughts and emotions without judgment. This authenticity is a key to unlocking deeper layers of self-awareness.

### B. Free-Writing and Stream of Consciousness:

Explore free-writing and stream-of-consciousness techniques. Allow your thoughts to flow without inhibition or concern for structure. This unfiltered expression often unveils hidden insights and emotions.

## 3. Navigating Emotions and Triggers:

### A. Emotional Awareness:

Use your journal to navigate and understand your emotions. When faced with challenges or triggers, write about your emotional responses. This process helps identify patterns, triggers, and the emotional roots of compulsive consumption.

## B. Tracking Patterns and Triggers:

Create a system for tracking patterns and triggers. Regularly reflect on your entries to identify recurring themes, situations, or emotions that precede binge episodes. This awareness is a crucial step toward breaking the cycle.

## 4. Setting Intentions and Goals:

### A. Clarity in Goal-Setting:

Journaling provides a platform to set clear intentions and goals. Define what you hope to achieve on your journey to lasting freedom from binge eating. Break down large goals into manageable steps and document your progress.

### B. Reflection on Progress:

Regularly reflect on your progress. Celebrate achievements, acknowledge challenges, and adjust goals as needed. Your journal becomes a dynamic record of your growth and a source of motivation.

## 5. Unraveling Thought Patterns:

### A. Cognitive Reflection:

Engage in cognitive reflection. Explore and challenge negative thought patterns that may contribute to binge eating. Use your journal to reframe these thoughts, fostering a more positive and empowering mindset.

### B. Identifying Distorted Beliefs:

Document and identify distorted beliefs. Journaling allows you to recognize and challenge irrational thoughts, creating space for healthier perspectives on food, self-image, and overall well-being.

**6. Mindful Reflection on Eating Habits:**

**A. Mindful Eating Journal:**

Create a mindful eating journal. Use it to record your eating experiences, paying attention to hunger cues, emotions associated with eating, and the sensations of each bite. Mindful reflection fosters a more conscious and intentional approach to food.

**B. Gratitude for Nourishment:**

Infuse gratitude into your reflections on food. Express appreciation for the nourishment your body receives. Cultivating gratitude shifts the focus from guilt or shame to a positive and nourishing relationship with food.

**7. Exploring Self-Compassion:**

**A. Compassionate Letters to Yourself:**

Incorporate self-compassion exercises. Write compassionate letters to yourself, acknowledging your efforts, strengths, and resilience. Cultivating self-compassion is a powerful antidote to the self-critical voices that may contribute to binge eating.

## B. Affirmations and Positive Reinforcement:

Integrate affirmations and positive reinforcement. Use your journal to reinforce positive qualities, experiences, and affirmations. This practice builds a foundation of self-empowerment and self-love.

## 8. Reflecting on Progress and Celebrating Victories:

### A. Progress Reflections:

Regularly reflect on your journey. Document moments of progress, no matter how small. Recognizing and celebrating victories, regardless of size, reinforces a positive and empowering narrative of your recovery.

**B. Celebration Rituals:**

Create celebration rituals for milestones. Establish rituals to acknowledge and celebrate your achievements, whether it's a special entry, a treat, or an activity you enjoy. These rituals become symbolic markers of your journey.

## Conclusion

Journaling is a profound tool for self-discovery and healing—a companion offering insights and self-compassion. This exploration invites you to embrace the transformative power of your words, unlocking the doors to a more profound understanding of yourself and the path to lasting freedom from binge eating.

# CHAPTER 12

# CULINARY EXPLORATION AND BINGE-FREE LIVING

Step into Chapter 12, a delectable journey into the world of culinary exploration—an invitation to savor the pleasures of food with mindfulness and joy on your path to lasting freedom from compulsive consumption.

In this chapter, we embark on a gastronomic adventure, celebrating the diverse flavors, textures, and aromas that enrich our relationship with food. Join me as we explore how culinary exploration becomes a key ingredient for a nourishing and binge-free life.

# HOW TO TRY NEW FOODS AND FLAVORS THAT EXPAND YOUR PALATE AND ENJOYMENT

Embarking on a journey to broaden your palate is not just about eating; it's a celebration of flavors, a dance with textures, and an exploration of the diverse world of cuisine.

In this chapter, we unravel the art of trying new foods and flavors, transforming your relationship with nourishment into a rich tapestry of culinary exploration.

Join me as we delve into practical strategies and mindful approaches to expand your palate, fostering a newfound enjoyment of food that aligns with your journey toward lasting freedom from compulsive consumption.

## 1. Cultivating a Curious Mindset:

### A. Embracing Openness:

Approach new foods with an open and curious mindset. Cultivate a sense of excitement about the discovery of flavors and textures. Embracing openness allows you to experience food with fresh eyes and an eager palate.

### B. Letting Go of Preconceptions:

Release preconceived notions about certain foods. Challenge yourself to approach each culinary experience without judgment or assumptions. This mental shift creates space for unbiased exploration.

## 2. Gradual Introduction of New Foods:

### A. Small Tasting Experiences:

Begin with small tasting experiences. Instead of committing to a full serving, take bite-sized portions to allow your palate to acclimate gradually. This approach minimizes the sense of overwhelm and encourages exploration.

**B. Incorporating Variety:**

Integrate variety into your meals. Aim to include a diverse range of foods in your daily diet, introducing new ingredients regularly. This approach broadens your palate, making the exploration process more accessible.

**3. Mindful Dining Practices:**

**A. Savoring Each Bite:**

Practice mindful eating. Pay attention to the flavors, textures, and aromas of each bite. Engage all your senses in the dining experience, creating a heightened awareness that enhances your enjoyment of new foods.

**B. Mindful Presence:**

Be present during meals. Minimize distractions, such as television or electronic devices, and focus on the sensory experience of eating. Mindful presence allows you to immerse yourself in the culinary adventure fully.

## 4. Exploring Different Cuisines:

### A. Global Culinary Exploration:

Explore different cuisines from around the world. Each culture brings a unique array of flavors and cooking techniques. Sampling dishes from diverse culinary traditions introduces you to exciting taste sensations.

### B. Ethnic Food Markets and Restaurants:

Visit ethnic food markets and restaurants. These venues provide authentic experiences, allowing you to immerse yourself in the richness of global flavors. Engage with the stories behind each dish for a more profound connection.

## 5. Cooking Adventures at Home:

**A. Trying New Recipes:**

Experiment with new recipes at home. Incorporate unfamiliar ingredients into your cooking repertoire, gradually expanding your culinary skills. Cooking becomes a creative and empowering expression of your culinary journey.

**B. Cooking Classes and Workshops:**

Participate in cooking classes or workshops. Learning from seasoned chefs or passionate cooks provides valuable insights into different cooking styles and introduces you to diverse ingredients.

## 6. Social Dining Experiences:

**A. Shared Culinary Adventures:**

Embark on culinary adventures with friends or family. Shared dining experiences create a social context for trying new foods, making exploring enjoyable and fostering a sense of community.

**B. Potluck Dinners:**

Organize potluck dinners. Invite friends to bring dishes from their favorite cuisines. This collaborative approach allows everyone to share and enjoy a variety of flavors, turning mealtime into a communal celebration.

## 7. Overcoming Food Fears:

### A. Gradual Exposure:

Address food fears through gradual exposure. Start with milder versions or variations of foods that may evoke anxiety. Gradual exposure and a positive mindset can help desensitize fears over time.

### B. Seeking Support:

If food fears persist, consider seeking support from a nutritionist or therapist. Professional guidance can provide personalized strategies for overcoming aversions and creating a more inclusive and enjoyable relationship with food.

# HOW TO EAT MINDFULLY AND APPRECIATE THE PLEASURES OF FOOD

Eating can become a hurried routine rather than a mindful experience in the bustling landscape of modern life. This chapter unfolds the art of mindful eating—an invitation to savor each bite, embrace the sensory delights of nourishment, and cultivate a deeper appreciation for the pleasures of food. Join me as we explore practical strategies and mindful approaches that transform your relationship with eating into a feast for the senses, aligning with your journey toward lasting freedom from compulsive consumption.

## 1. Cultivating Present-Moment Awareness:

### A. Eliminating Distractions:

Create a mindful eating environment by eliminating distractions. Turn off electronic devices, step away from work, and create a serene space dedicated to eating. This intentional setting allows you to focus on the sensory experience.

### B. Engaging the Five Senses:

Activate all five senses during meals. Notice the colors, textures, and aromas of your food. Listen to the sounds of cooking or the crunch of a crisp vegetable. Engaging the senses enhances present-moment awareness.

## 2. Developing a Gratitude Practice:

### A. Pre-Meal Reflection:

Take a moment for pre-meal reflection. Express gratitude for the nourishment before you. This practice shifts your mindset from routine consumption to a moment of appreciation for the gift of food.

**B. Expressing Gratitude During Meals:**

Incorporate gratitude into your eating experience. As you consume each bite, express gratitude for the flavors and sustenance. This intentional focus enhances the positive connection between your mind and the act of eating.

## 3. Slow and Intentional Eating:

### A. Mindful Chewing:

Chew each bite mindfully and thoroughly. Pay attention to the textures and flavors as you chew. Mindful chewing not only aids digestion but also allows you to savor the intricacies of your meal.

**B. Setting Utensils Down:**

Practice setting utensils down between bites. This intentional pause prevents rushed eating and encourages a more deliberate and mindful approach to each morsel.

## 4. Listening to Hunger and Fullness Cues:

### A. Tune into Hunger Signals:

Before eating, tune into your body's hunger signals. Ask yourself if you're genuinely hungry or responding to emotional cues. Mindful awareness of hunger enhances your eating ability in response to genuine physical needs.

### B. Recognizing Fullness:

Pay attention to feelings of fullness during meals. Pause periodically to assess your satiety levels. Mindful recognition of fullness helps prevent overeating and promotes a more balanced relationship with food.

## 5. Mindful Portion Control:

### A. Serving Sizes and Plate Composition:

Be mindful of portion sizes and plate composition. Serve reasonable portions, considering the nutritional balance of your meal. Mindful portion control supports conscious and intentional eating.

### B. Savoring Small Bites:

Deliberately savor small bites. Rather than rushing through a meal, take the time to appreciate the flavors and textures of each morsel. This approach transforms eating into a pleasurable and mindful experience.

## 6. Mindful Food Choices:

### A. Conscious Ingredient Selection:

Select ingredients consciously. Consider the nutritional value, freshness, and quality of your foods. Mindful food choices contribute to a holistic and nourishing eating experience.

## B. Exploring Diverse Flavors:

Experiment with diverse flavors and cuisines. Mindful eating involves expanding your palate and appreciating the richness of different tastes. This exploration adds a layer of excitement and enjoyment to your meals.

## 7. Post-Meal Reflection:

### A. Reflecting on Satisfaction:

After finishing a meal, reflect on your level of satisfaction. Were you truly nourished, both physically and emotionally? This post-meal reflection reinforces a positive connection between mindful eating and overall well-being.

### B. Gratitude for the Culinary Experience:

Express gratitude for the culinary experience. Whether you prepared the meal or enjoyed it at a restaurant, acknowledging the effort and artistry involved in creating nourishing food enhances your appreciation for the pleasures of eating.

## Conclusion

Culinary exploration and mindful eating intertwine in a sensory journey, transcending mere consumption. Embrace the joy, curiosity, and satisfaction in each bite. This exploration invites you to savor life's diverse flavors, enhancing enjoyment on the path to lasting freedom from compulsive consumption—a dynamic, intuitive journey guided by intention and profound appreciation for nourishment.

# CHAPTER 13

# HOLISTIC MIND-BODY HEALING AND BINGE-FREE LIVING

Welcome to Chapter 13, a sanctuary for integrating mind and body—a journey into holistic healing on your path to lasting freedom from compulsive consumption. This chapter explores the interconnected realms of mental and physical well-being, unveiling the transformative power of holistic approaches that nurture wholeness.

Join me as we navigate the landscape of holistic mind-body healing, embracing practices that harmonize the intricate dance between your mental and physical selves for enduring liberation from the shadows of binge eating.

# HOW TO INCORPORATE COMPLEMENTARY THERAPIES THAT ENHANCE YOUR HEALTH AND WELLBEING

In pursuing lasting freedom from binge eating, this chapter unfolds a tapestry of complementary therapies—a holistic embrace of practices that extend beyond traditional approaches to foster overall health and well-being. Join me as we explore diverse modalities that synergize with conventional methods, providing a comprehensive toolkit for healing and enhancing your physical, mental, and emotional balance on the journey to lasting liberation from compulsive consumption.

## 1. Embracing Mindfulness Meditation:

### A. Mindful Awareness Practices:

Incorporate mindfulness meditation into your daily routine. Engage in practices that cultivate present-moment awareness, such as guided meditation, mindful breathing, or body scan exercises. Mindfulness promotes mental clarity, emotional balance, and an enhanced connection with your body.

### B. Meditation Apps and Resources:

Explore meditation apps and online resources. Platforms offering guided meditations can be valuable companions on your journey, providing structured sessions catering to mental and emotional well-being.

## 2. Exploring Yoga for Mind-Body Harmony:

### A. Gentle Yoga Practices:

Integrate gentle yoga into your exercise routine. Yoga promotes flexibility, strength, and a sense of inner calm. Choose practices such as Hatha or Yin yoga that emphasize mindfulness and the connection between breath and movement.

### B. Yoga Classes or Online Sessions:

Attend yoga classes or explore online sessions. Participating in guided classes, whether in-person or virtually, introduces you to structured sequences that enhance both physical fitness and mental relaxation.

## 2. Harnessing the Power of Acupuncture:

### A. Traditional Chinese Medicine Approach:

Consider acupuncture as part of your holistic approach. Rooted in traditional Chinese medicine, acupuncture involves the insertion of thin needles into specific points on the body to promote energy flow. This modality can aid in stress reduction and overall balance.

**B. Consultation with Acupuncturists:**

Seek the guidance of licensed acupuncturists. Professional consultations ensure that acupuncture is tailored to your specific needs, addressing your journey's physical and emotional aspects.

**3. Integrating Massage Therapy:**

**A. Relaxation and Stress Reduction:**

Incorporate massage therapy for relaxation and stress reduction. Therapeutic massage techniques can alleviate tension, promote circulation, and provide a nurturing space for your body to heal.

**B. Different Massage Modalities:**

Explore various massage modalities. From Swedish to deep tissue massage, each approach offers unique benefits. Choose a modality that aligns with your preferences and complements your wellness plan.

## 4. Engaging in Art and Expressive Therapies:

### A. Artistic Expression for Emotional Release:

Explore art and expressive therapies as tools for emotional release. Engaging in activities like painting, drawing, or creative writing provides an outlet for self-expression and processing emotions.

### B. Art Therapy Professionals:

Consider working with art therapists. Trained professionals can guide you through therapeutic creative processes, helping you explore and understand your emotions in a supportive and non-verbal manner.

## 5. Holistic Nutrition Counseling:

### A. Personalized Nutritional Guidance:

Seek holistic nutrition counseling. Work with professionals considering your overall health and lifestyle to craft a personalized nutrition plan. Holistic nutrition addresses dietary choices and the relationship between food and your body's unique needs.

### B. Mindful Eating Practices:

Integrate mindful eating practices into your nutritional approach. Listen to hunger cues, savor flavors, and make conscious food choices. Mindful eating enhances your awareness of the nourishing qualities of food.

## 6. Herbal and Nutritional Supplements:

**A. Consultation with Healthcare Professionals:**

Consider herbal and nutritional supplements under the guidance of healthcare professionals. Certain supplements may complement your overall wellness plan, addressing nutritional deficiencies or supporting specific health goals.

**B. Natural Remedies for Stress and Anxiety:**

Explore natural remedies for stress and anxiety. Herbs like chamomile, lavender, or adaptogenic supplements provide gentle support for emotional well-being when incorporated into your routine.

**7. Aromatherapy for Emotional Balance:**

**A. Essential Oils for Wellbeing:**

Incorporate aromatherapy into your daily rituals. Essential oils such as lavender, peppermint, or citrus blends can create a calming atmosphere, promoting emotional balance and relaxation.

**B. Diffusers and Topical Application:**
Use diffusers or apply diluted essential oils topically. Experiment with different scents to find combinations that resonate with your senses, enhancing your mental and emotional state.

# HOW TO USE HOLISTIC APPROACHES TO HEAL YOUR PHYSICAL AND MENTAL WOUNDS

In the intricate tapestry of healing, this chapter unfolds the art of holistic approaches—an exploration of practices that address not only the physical but also the mental and emotional wounds on your path to lasting recovery from compulsive consumption. Join me as we delve into comprehensive strategies, embracing a holistic perspective that nurtures wholeness and fosters profound healing for your entire being.

## 1. Mind-Body Practices for Stress Reduction:

### A. Mindfulness Meditation:

Initiate a daily mindfulness meditation practice. Mindfulness cultivates awareness of the present moment, reducing stress and promoting mental clarity. Regular practice serves as a foundation for healing both physical and emotional wounds.

### B. Progressive Muscle Relaxation (PMR):

Explore Progressive Muscle Relaxation (PMR). This technique involves systematically tensing and releasing different muscle groups, promoting physical relaxation and reducing stress.

**2. Yoga for Physical and Emotional Wellbeing:**

**A. Yoga for Emotional Release:**

Engage in yoga practices that emphasize emotional release. Poses such as Child's Pose, Pigeon Pose, and Savasana provide a space for emotional expression and help release tension stored in the body.

**B. Yoga Nidra for Mental Healing:**

Incorporate Yoga Nidra for mental healing. Also known as "yogic sleep," this guided meditation technique promotes deep relaxation and can be a powerful tool for addressing mental wounds and fostering inner peace.

**3. Integrative Bodywork Therapies:**

**A. Massage Therapy for Emotional Release:**

Integrate massage therapy as a form of emotional release. Massage addresses physical tension and provides a safe space to release emotional stress stored in the body.

## B. Craniosacral Therapy for Mind-Body Connection:

Consider Craniosacral Therapy. This gentle form of bodywork focuses on the craniosacral system and helps restore balance to the body, fostering a deeper mind-body connection.

## 4. Holistic Nutrition for Physical Restoration:

### A. Whole Foods and Nutrient-Rich Diet:

Adopt a whole foods and nutrient-rich diet. Holistic nutrition emphasizes the importance of nourishing your body with foods supporting overall health and aiding in physical healing.

### B. Anti-Inflammatory Foods:

Explore anti-inflammatory foods. Incorporate foods rich in antioxidants, omega-3 fatty acids, and phytonutrients to combat inflammation, supporting physical and mental healing.

## 5. Herbal Remedies and Adaptogens:

### A. Herbal Teas for Calming:

Incorporate herbal teas for calming effects. Chamomile, lavender, and passionflower teas have soothing properties that can contribute to mental relaxation and emotional balance.

### B. Adaptogenic Herbs for Stress Resilience:

Explore adaptogenic herbs for stress resilience. Herbs like ashwagandha, rhodiola, and holy basil help the body adapt to stressors, supporting physical and mental resilience.

**6. Art and Expressive Therapies for Emotional Expression:**

**A. Art Therapy for Emotional Release:**

Engage in art therapy for emotional expression. Creative activities such as painting, drawing, or sculpting provide a non-verbal outlet for processing and releasing emotional wounds.

**B. Music Therapy for Mood Regulation:**

Consider music therapy for mood regulation. Listening to or creating music can profoundly impact emotional states, contributing to a sense of emotional balance and healing.

**7. Cognitive-behavioral therapy (CBT) for Mental Well-being:**

**A. Identifying and Challenging Negative Thoughts:**

Embrace Cognitive-Behavioral Therapy (CBT) principles. Work on identifying and challenging negative thought patterns that may contribute to mental wounds, fostering a more positive and adaptive mindset.

### B. Mindfulness-Based Cognitive Therapy (MBCT):

Explore Mindfulness-Based Cognitive Therapy (MBCT). This approach integrates mindfulness practices into traditional CBT, enhancing awareness and promoting mental well-being.

## 8. Holistic Approaches to Trauma Recovery:

### A. Trauma-Informed Yoga:

Consider trauma-informed yoga. Tailored to individuals with a history of trauma, this approach to yoga emphasizes safety, choice, and empowerment in the healing process.

### B. EMDR (Eye Movement Desensitization and Reprocessing):

Explore EMDR as a holistic approach to trauma recovery. This therapeutic technique involves bilateral stimulation to process traumatic memories, fostering healing on a mental and emotional level.

## Conclusion

Complementary therapies and holistic approaches integrate mind, body, and spirit, offering a personalized plan for lasting liberation. This exploration invites you to embrace these practices as tools for enduring recovery, weaving them into your daily life for holistic healing.

# CHAPTER 14

# EMPOWERING YOUR BINGE-FREE LIVING JOURNEY

Step into Chapter 14, a beacon of empowerment on your journey to lasting freedom from compulsive consumption. This chapter is a testament to your strength and resilience—a guide to unleashing the power within you to overcome obstacles and emerge victorious. Join me as we explore strategies, mindset shifts, and tools that empower you on your binge-free living journey, turning challenges into stepping stones toward lasting liberation.

# HOW TO BUILD RESILIENCE AND SELF-EMPOWERMENT THAT SUPPORT YOUR BINGE-FREE LIVING

In the realm of lasting liberation from compulsive consumption, resilience, and self-empowerment emerge as stalwart companions, guiding your path through challenges toward enduring freedom. This chapter serves as a compass, illuminating strategies and practices that fortify your inner strength and empower you to navigate the complexities of your binge-free living journey.

## 1. Cultivating a Growth Mindset:

### A. Embracing Challenges as Opportunities:

Adopt a growth mindset by viewing challenges as opportunities for learning and growth. Shift your perspective to see setbacks not as failures but as stepping stones toward personal development on your journey to lasting liberation.

**B. Fostering Positive Self-Talk:**

Develop positive self-talk habits. Challenge negative thoughts and replace them with affirmations reinforcing your resilience and ability to overcome obstacles. Cultivating a positive inner dialogue bolsters your self-empowerment.

**2. Setting Realistic and Meaningful Goals:**

**A. SMART Goal Setting:**

Establish SMART (Specific, Measurable, Achievable, Relevant, Time-bound) goals. Break down your binge-free living objectives into actionable and realistic steps. Setting clear goals provides a roadmap for progress and enhances your sense of self-efficacy.

**B. Aligning Goals with Personal Values:**

Ensure your goals align with your values. Meaningful objectives rooted in your values motivate you and deepen your connection to the purpose behind your journey, fostering long-term commitment.

**3. Resilience through Mindfulness Practices:**

**A. Mindful Coping Strategies:**

Incorporate mindfulness practices to build resilience. Techniques such as mindful breathing and meditation enhance your ability to navigate stressors with a calm and centered mindset. Mindfulness becomes a tool for resilience in the face of challenges.

**B. Acceptance and Commitment Therapy (ACT):**

Explore Acceptance and Commitment Therapy (ACT). This therapeutic approach encourages acceptance of difficult emotions while committing to actions aligned with your values. ACT empowers you to move forward despite challenges.

**4. Building a Support Network:**

**A. Identifying Supportive Individuals:**

Surround yourself with a supportive network. Identify individuals who understand and encourage your journey toward lasting freedom. Building a support system provides a safety net during challenging times, reinforcing your resilience.

**B. Sharing Your Journey:**

Openly share your experiences with trusted friends or family. Voicing your challenges and triumphs fosters connection and allows others to contribute to your empowerment, creating a shared sense of resilience.

## 5. Self-Compassion Practices:

### A. Embracing Self-Compassion:

Practice self-compassion. Treat yourself with the same kindness and understanding you would offer a friend facing difficulties. Cultivating self-compassion fosters resilience by providing a nurturing internal environment.

### B. Learning from Setbacks:

View setbacks as opportunities for growth, not as indications of personal failure. Extract lessons from challenges and use them to inform your approach moving forward. Every setback becomes a stepping stone toward greater resilience.

## 6. Skill-Building for Emotional Regulation:

### A. Identifying Triggers and Coping Strategies:

Enhance emotional regulation by identifying triggers and developing coping strategies. Understanding the root causes of emotional challenges empowers you to respond proactively, reinforcing your resilience in the face of emotional turmoil.

### B. Developing Emotional Intelligence:

Cultivate emotional intelligence. Strengthening your ability to recognize and manage emotions not only supports your mental health but also enhances your resilience in navigating the emotional complexities of your binge-free living journey.

## 7. Celebrating Milestones and Progress:

### A. Acknowledging Achievements:

Celebrate milestones, no matter how small. Acknowledge and reward yourself for the progress made on your journey. Regularly recognizing your achievements bolsters your sense of empowerment and reinforces positive behaviors.

### B. Reflecting on Growth:

Take time to reflect on your personal growth. Recognize the changes, both internal and external, that signify progress. This reflective practice reinforces your resilience by highlighting the positive evolution on your binge-free living journey.

# HOW TO INSPIRE OTHERS THROUGH YOUR BINGE-FREE LIVING STORY AND EXPERIENCE

As you stand on the precipice of lasting liberation from compulsive consumption, your journey becomes more than a personal triumph—a source of inspiration for others seeking their path to freedom. This chapter explores the art of sharing your binge-free living story and experience, transforming your challenges into a beacon of hope that illuminates the way for others on their unique journeys.

**1. Crafting Your Authentic Narrative:**

**A. Reflecting on Your Journey:**

Take time to reflect on your binge-free living journey. Identify key moments, challenges, and triumphs that have shaped your experience. This reflection forms the foundation for crafting an authentic and relatable narrative.

**B. Honoring Vulnerability:**

Embrace vulnerability in your storytelling. Share the raw and genuine aspects of your journey—the struggles, doubts, and moments of uncertainty. Honoring vulnerability creates a connection with others facing similar challenges.

**2. Identifying Universal Themes:**

**A. Common Struggles and Triumphs:**

Identify universal themes in your experience. Highlight common struggles that resonate with many individuals dealing with binge eating and the triumphs that showcase the potential for lasting liberation.

### B. Relatable Emotions:

Express relatable emotions. Connect with your audience by articulating the emotional aspects of your journey. Whether it's the frustration of setbacks or the joy of milestones, relatable emotions forge a deep connection.

### 3. Tailoring Your Message to Your Audience:

#### A. Understanding Your Audience:

Consider your target audience. Tailor your message to resonate with the experiences and concerns of those seeking inspiration. Understanding your audience enhances the impact of your storytelling.

#### B. Empathy and Compassion:

Approach your audience with empathy and compassion. Acknowledge the challenges they may be facing and offer understanding. Creating a supportive and compassionate space fosters a sense of unity and shared understanding.

## 4. Utilizing Different Mediums:

### A. Written Narratives:

Craft written narratives to share your story. Blogs, articles, or personal essays provide platforms for in-depth exploration of your journey. Written mediums allow for detailed expression and reflection.

### B. Visual Storytelling:

Explore visual storytelling through mediums like videos or presentations. Visual elements add depth to your narrative, allowing your audience to connect with your journey's visual and emotional aspects.

## 5. Offering Practical Insights:

### A. Lessons Learned:

Share practical insights and lessons learned. Offer tips and strategies that have been instrumental in your binge-free living journey. Providing actionable advice adds value and guidance for others.

**B. Encouraging Self-Reflection:**

Encourage self-reflection in your audience. Pose questions or prompts that prompt individuals to consider their experiences and take proactive steps toward their unique paths to lasting liberation.

## 6. Emphasizing Growth and Resilience:

### A. Showcasing Personal Growth:

Highlight your personal growth throughout the journey. Emphasize the transformative aspects of your experience, showcasing how challenges have become growth opportunities.

### B. Resilience in the Face of Setbacks:

Illustrate resilience in the face of setbacks. Share instances where you navigated challenges and emerged stronger. Emphasizing resilience provides hope and encouragement for those encountering obstacles.

## 7. Fostering Community and Connection:

### A. Creating Supportive Spaces:

Establish supportive communities or spaces where individuals can share their stories. Fostering a sense of community creates a platform for shared experiences and mutual support.

### B. Engaging with Your Audience:

Actively engage with your audience. Respond to comments, questions, and messages with empathy and encouragement. This interactive approach fosters a sense of connection and solidarity.

## <u>Conclusion</u>

Building resilience and self-empowerment unfolds in your journey toward lasting liberation from compulsive consumption. Empowerment is not a destination but an evolving practice—an invitation to cultivate resilience and inner strength. Simultaneously, your binge-free living story is a gift of hope and inspiration, illuminating the path for others. This exploration invites you to weave your narrative into the collective tapestry of resilience, empowering others on their unique journeys toward lasting freedom.

# CONCLUSION

As you reach the end of this transformative journey through the chapters of **"Binge-Free Living,"** I want to express my deepest gratitude for embarking on this exploration with me. From understanding the intricacies of compulsive eating to unraveling the profound connection between mind and body, each chapter has been a stepping stone toward holistic well-being.

In these pages, we've delved into the roots of emotional wellness, balanced the dance between movement and rest, and cultivated a supportive environment for your binge-free living journey. Meal planning, goal-setting, seeking professional guidance—all **essential** components intricately **woven** into the tapestry of your lasting liberation.

From the vibrant palette of culinary exploration to the profound self-discovery facilitated by mindful reflection and journaling, we've embraced holistic self-care and holistic mind-body healing. The journey has empowered you to build resilience, create milestones, and inspire others through your unique story.

As you stand at the threshold of empowerment and enduring freedom, I encourage you to reflect on your growth, celebrate your successes, and acknowledge the strength that brought you here. This isn't just the end of a book; it's the beginning of a new chapter in **your** life.

I invite you to continue practicing the principles you've discovered, making them a seamless part of your daily routine. Your journey doesn't end with the last page; it extends into each mindful bite, every moment of self-care, and the profound connections you foster.

If **"TransformBinge-Free Living"** has resonated with you, I kindly ask for your feedback and reviews. Your insights could be the guiding light for others seeking their path to liberation. Remember, your journey is a beacon, inspiring others toward their binge-free living.

As you move forward, continue your practice, celebrate your victories, and inspire those around you. This isn't just a book; it's a roadmap to lasting transformation. **Thank you for allowing me to be part of your journey.**

**Wishing you joy, fulfillment, and enduring freedom,**

[Unique Kade]